DANCING in the DUNGEON

Suffering With Hopeful Joy For God's Glory

Alicia, 3-1-15

MAY YOU WALK IN GOD'S COMFORT.

Ron Ethridge Jr.

CROSSBOOKS

CrossBooks™
A Division of LifeWay
1663 Liberty Drive
Bloomington, IN 47403
www.crossbooks.com
Phone: 1-866-879-0502

© 2014 Ron Ethridge Jr.. All rights reserved.

No part of this book may be reproduced, stored in a retrieval system, or transmitted by any means without the written permission of the author.

Scripture quotations are from The Holy Bible, English Standard Version® (ESV®), copyright © 2001 by Crossway, a publishing ministry of Good News Publishers. Used by permission. All rights reserved.

First published by CrossBooks 02/14/2014

ISBN: 978-1-4627-3499-3 (sc)
ISBN: 978-1-4627-3498-6 (hc)
ISBN: 978-1-4627-3500-6 (e)

Library of Congress Control Number: 2014902625

Printed in the United States of America.

This book is printed on acid-free paper.

Any people depicted in stock imagery provided by Thinkstock are models, and such images are being used for illustrative purposes only. Certain stock imagery © Thinkstock.

Because of the dynamic nature of the Internet, any web addresses or links contained in this book may have changed since publication and may no longer be valid. The views expressed in this work are solely those of the author and do not necessarily reflect the views of the publisher, and the publisher hereby disclaims any responsibility for them.

Unless otherwise noted, all scripture quotations are from The Holy Bible, English Standard Version® (ESV®), copyright © 2001 by Crossway, a publishing ministry of Good News Publishers. Used by permission. All rights reserved.

CONTENTS

Endorsements vii
Foreword ix
Preface xiii
Introduction xxi

Chapter 1   What God Can Do 1
Chapter 2   A Theology of Encouragement 15
Chapter 3   Heaven… The Best Is Yet to Come 35
Chapter 4   Why Me, Why This, Why Now 46
Chapter 5   When God Is Silent 59
Chapter 6   Prayer… Your Desire Is God's Will 72
Chapter 7   Attitude and Rest for the Soul 91
Chapter 8   Comfort When Betrayed 100
Chapter 9   Comfort in Personal Failure 110
Chapter 10 When Sheep Attack Shepherds 129
Chapter 11 When and How to Terminate a Minister 153
Chapter 12 Now What? 165

Afterword 167
Appendix A 169
About The Author 171
Endnotes 173

ENDORSEMENTS

. . . .

The problem of suffering has always haunted Christians. If you are a follower of Christ, why do you suffer? The answer to that age-old question is not easy, but it may be obvious. Because we are followers of Christ, we experience suffering.

Ron Ethridge has transformed his story of dealing with suffering into a book that is a helpful guide for all of us. *Dancing in the Dungeon* is a personal story. Ron is very transparent in telling about those moments when he suffered most in life. He does so knowing that our God can use suffering for His glory. That is the theme of this book.

Not only is *Dancing in the Dungeon* personal in nature, it's biblical in content and practical in application. As a fellow sufferer, you find comfort and hope in the pages of this book. You will be encouraged to worship, pray, and serve our Lord even in the midst of suffering.

I am grateful that Ron Ethridge has shared his story and the redemptive lessons that can be learned from it. Experiences of suffering can be and should be a laboratory of learning for Christ followers.

Dr. Rick Lance
Executive Director
Alabama Baptist Convention

***

We all go through hard times. As Ron Ethridge wisely reminds us, no one gets a free ride through life. That certainly includes pastors who serve in vocational ministry. If that's the bad news, then the good news is that God uses those hard times for our good and His glory. *Dancing in the Dungeon* takes us to the ragged edge of life to show us that, when we feel most forgotten, God is doing His best work in us. Of all the good things about this book, the best is that Ron brings us back again and again to the Bible so we will discover what God has said about the hard times of life. Read it so you will be equipped when your time comes to dance in the dungeon.

Dr. Ray Pritchard
President, Keep Believing Ministries
Author of *An Anchor for the Soul*, *The Healing Power of Forgiveness*, and *He's God and We're Not*

FOREWORD

. . . .

When you pass through the waters, I will be with you; and through the rivers, they shall not overwhelm you; when you walk through fire you shall not be burned, and the flame shall not consume you. But I am the Lord your God, the holy one of Israel, your Savior" (Isa. 43:2-3).

These words from the prophet Isaiah were first addressed to the people of Israel to remind them that God's covenant-love would sustain them in the midst of life's hardest difficulties. But they also apply to believers today, including pastors, who sometimes find themselves walking through unexpected flames they are not prepared for.

Ron Ethridge is an ordained Baptist minister whose past service in the church follows a well-trodden trajectory. Brought up in the church, followed by undergraduate studies in a denominational setting, and then seminary at a fine theological school, Ron was ready to pursue a life of pastoral ministry in fulfillment of what he was sure was God's calling on his life. Then, midstream, Ron found himself on the outside of the church looking in when he was asked to leave two of the churches he had been called to serve. Rather than precipitate a knock-down floor fight at the church business meeting, Ron decided to walk away.

Ron admits that he himself made mistakes along the way and that, in hindsight, he would do some things quite differently. This book is not about victimhood or retaliation. Rather, it is the anguished cry of a wounded shepherd, one who has come to understand that healing only happens in the broken places. Through Redemption Ministry, Ron Ethridge is now reaching out to all who are hurting with an emphasis on fellow ministers who find themselves the situation of conflict, and possibly termination, on that part of God's flock they have been called to serve. Ron wants to come alongside his fellow struggling pastors and hurting Christians to offer encouragement and counsel.

There are certainly times when a minister should—and must—be removed from his place of service. But this should be done only in extreme circumstances, with careful deliberation, and with prayer and wise counsel offered by respected leaders within and beyond the local congregation. Too often today the pattern of forced pastoral termination does not meet these criteria. The landscape is littered with pastors and churches whose relationships have been severed in ways that can only make the devil smile.

This issue—and this book—raise searching questions. Is the problem one of polity or church governance? In Methodist church life bishops play an oversight role among pastors and congregations. Presbyterians have elders, presbyteries, and committees of discipline. Some denominations offer programs of intentional rehabilitation and restoration for ministers who find themselves in a pastoral crisis. Baptists and other free church Christians usually place a large share of responsibility in the hands of the congregation. They do so because they believe (rightly, in my view) that this pattern of church life most faithfully represents the New Testament model. Yet the question remains: In our present culture, is this pattern susceptible to misuse and abuse?

My own view is that, at the end of the day, the issue is not one of church polity but of spirituality. We need to follow a more biblical method of resolving congregational conflict. We need repentance. We need revival.

Jesus prayed that his disciples would be one, even as he and the Father were one, so that the world might believe (John 17:21). Jesus also gave his disciples a new commandment—that they love one another, just as he had loved them. "By this," Jesus said, "All people will know that you are my disciples, if you have love for one another" (John 13:34-35). Many people are hurt when things blow up in the life of the church. There is always collateral damage when conflict among God's people erupts—the pastor, his family, the congregation, the denomination. But more serious than any of these is the impact such actions have on those who do not know Jesus Christ as Lord and Savior. Jesus said that those on the outside, those in the world, would know that his followers truly belong to him by their observable love for one another. How else are they to know? They cannot read our minds or see into our hearts but they can listen to our lips, observe our lives, and see how we treat one another in our words and actions.

In all that we say and do on behalf of the cause of Christ, nothing is more important than to bear the true mark of the Christian—so that the world might believe.

Dr. Timothy George
Founding Dean of Beeson Divinity School
and chairman of the board of the Chuck Colson Center
for Christian Worldview.

PREFACE

. . . .

And the Hits Just Keep on Coming[1]

Joy, contentment, peace, blessings, and happiness are God's will for every believer in Christ. I'm certain those things are His will for all who believe, without exception. Why else would it be recorded in God's Word that Jesus said, "I came that they may have life and have it abundantly" (John 10:10). Consider therefore the following truths and be encouraged.

- "Blessed are you when people hate you and when they exclude you and revile you and spurn your name as evil, on account of the Son of Man! Rejoice in that day, and leap for joy, for behold, your reward is great in heaven; for so their fathers did to the prophets" (Luke 6:22–23).
- "These things I have spoken to you, that my joy may be in you, and that your joy may be full" (John 15:11)
- "Ask, and you will receive, that your joy may be full" (John 16:24)
- "I am coming to you, and these things I speak in the world, that they may have my joy fulfilled in themselves" (John 17:13)
- "Peace I leave with you; my peace I give to you. Not as the world gives do I give to you. Let not your hearts be troubled, neither let them be afraid." (John 14:27)

The goal of *Dancing in the Dungeon* is for the believer to experience these promises of Jesus. My hope is for believers to be strengthened in their view of God and their faith in Him and, as a result, live a life of contentment, peace, and joy. I pray the God of all comfort will comfort them as they reflect on Him as He reveals his ways, purposes, thoughts, and promises from Scripture. Then as a result, what is written in 2 Corinthians 1:3–4 will be fulfilled.

> Blessed be the God and Father of our Lord Jesus Christ, the Father of mercies and God of all comfort, who comforts us in all our affliction, so that we may be able to comfort those who are in any affliction, with the comfort with which we ourselves are comforted by God.

I pray God will use and redeem your difficulties by comforting others who are afflicted through you. Always be looking for hurting people around you. God will show them to you so you can bring His comfort into their lives. It is God's will for His mercy and grace to be spread by His people to others for His glory.

After all is said and done, God is the only comfort and source of comfort. Therefore, I encourage reading the endnotes because they point to God's Word, which is much more important than anything that the author has written. Each scripture referenced to an endnote is for encouragement of the Scripture. As it is written in Romans 15:4, "For whatever was written in former days was written for our instruction, that through endurance and through the encouragement of the Scriptures we might have hope."

Because hope and peace is promised for believers, why is there so much pain and brokenness in Christians' lives? Part of the answer is found in John 14:27, "Not as the world gives." The kind of peace and joy Jesus gives is different from the world's. Jesus' peace and joy is opposite of how most people expect to receive peace and joy. *Dancing in the Dungeon* is written for Christians to embrace the unexpected way that God increases joy, peace, and contentment. Thus, the reader should anticipate contemporary American perspectives to be challenged regarding how his or her best life now takes place.

Understanding Our Situation

Because of sin, every family and person in a family is dysfunctional. It's just a matter of degree and kind. Dysfunctions are the result of every generation being wounded by their parents and passing along wounds to their children. We are broken people raised by broken parents who live in a broken world trying to raise children born broken.[2] Wounding others is not intentional. It is what people living in a world massively sickened by the cancer of sin do. The only way anyone is healed is when God does it His way in His time through the Holy Spirit and Jesus Christ's blood.[3]

When I once needed emergency surgery, I didn't want a first-year resident holding a scalpel for the first time. I wanted an experienced physician to perform the procedure successfully. Likewise, when I needed help with life problems, I wanted to hear from—and listened most closely to—those who had walked with God through the furnace of affliction. Notice I didn't want a person who walked with God, but one who walked with Him through the furnace of affliction. Experience is the best teacher and lends credibility to people, their insights, and recommendations.

What follows are some of my life experiences for the reader to determine if what I've written has a measure of credibility. Those who read this have suffered more than I have while others suffer less. My hardships don't rise to the level of real suffering for the gospel,[4] but they are mine nonetheless. My deepest wounds are in the context of family, while the greater number was while serving as a pastor. Regardless of the source, wounds leave scars. I was not taught how to process hardships, which resulted in often feeling hopeless; however, God comforted me by bringing many resources and people into my life over the course of decades. I pray through my experiences that God will comfort you.

My Story

From the age of four, my alcoholic dad exposed me to conversations and situations of immoral nature no child should ever see, hear, or encounter. He exposed me to the occult in the forms of the satanic bible (not capitalized on purpose), Ouija board, hypnotism, and out-of-body experiences. He and his brother put me in situations I won't describe, but they deeply wounded my psyche and soul. Except for God's grace, those things could have driven me to living a decadent life. My dad was not a believer at the time, and he did love me. He just had major character flaws from which God sovereignly protected me.

I had a physiological disorder that resulted in being publicly ashamed, having my peers shun me, and feeling embarrassed often from age five to thirteen. After God saved me at the age of ten, my dad continued abusing alcohol with anger issues and mistreatment of my mom, all of which continued once he became a pastor.[5] Consequently, I was somewhat conflicted about Christianity because of how my dad lived, in particular to how he treated my mom. During my middle teen years, I struggled to understand why God would allow all those things. Then while in college, I wondered why God would cause/allow me to lose a childhood dream.[6]

The greatest number of wounds I have experienced was while serving as a pastor.[7] All the accusations toward my family and me were untrue and/or proven to be false. I admit I have not been perfect and made mistakes I regret. I do lament giving people sticks to beat me with from my own ignorance and foolishness. Yet by God's grace, none of my failures was of immoral nature, doctrinal heresy, or breaking the law.

The first three churches I served fired the pastor prior to me, which means I entered seriously conflicted situations.[8] In the space of eighteen months prior to my arrival, one church fired the youth pastor, pressured a pastor to resign, and then forced the worship leader to resign.[9] In one church, during the second week after becoming senior pastor, two staff members began relating to me the failures and mistakes of other and previous staff, which exposed the negative attitude in the church as a whole.[10] One congregation pressured five of their six pastors to resign.[11] Over four decades, another church I served pressured five of seven pastors prior to me to resign, which did not include support staff who were pressured to resign.[12]

After being in ministry a while and observing firsthand the hurt and pain in congregations that had terminated ministers, along with how communities viewed them as dysfunctional, I made a philosophical decision. I decided, if I were ever in a situation that disintegrated into significant disharmony, rather than stay and be a part of a public church fight and split, I would resign in the prayerful hope that leaving would help protect the name of Christ and the reputation of the Christian faith and congregation and hopefully speed healing.[13] I never thought I would have to make that decision… twice.

A deacon in the first church I served told me that he'd either see me dead or run off, so he nicknamed me "Little Hitler."[14] Another man called me Lucifer while yet another, a retired pastor, told church members I had followed Satan's call to be the pastor rather than following God's call.[15] One time, petitions were circulated for another staff member and me to be fired. A deacon in this church proudly told many members about his work to have me terminated, "I will either be the biggest hero or goat this church has ever seen."

At two churches, it was told my wife and I was separated because of marital problems. Both my wife and I had been accused of having affairs. My children have been accused of immoral behavior with it being rumored one of them had to get married.[16] I was accused of using the church credit card for personal means, having pornography on my blog, acting like a homosexual with another minister at a funeral, and trying to run off staff. I was told in a deacon's meeting that there were irreconcilable differences between church leaders and me, but the men refused to tell me what the differences were so they could be addressed.[17]

A personnel team chairman told church members that a state worker warned him I had a reputation of being a manipulator and for the church to do whatever they had to do in order to prevent it from happening.[18] A female staff member accused me of making physical threats, which another staff member present at the event argued it did not happen.[19] In this congregation, I asked the chairman of deacons to set up a meeting with two people who had issues with me because I wanted to work toward restoration and reconciliation; however, they told him, "We don't want restoration or reconciliation. We want him gone." Then I was accused at two churches of not preaching Baptist doctrine.[20]

Like most ministers, I have had my share of anonymous accusatory letters, emails, and phone calls. The hardest thing to deal with was those who did these things were my brothers and sisters in Christ whom I loved deeply.[21]

Then over the years, I have battled mild depression. The events recounted from my church experiences are representative of many things not related here, as most ministers can attest to from their own experiences.[22]

At the same time, I must say with great joy that, in every congregation, God has provided people who loved Jesus, were encouragers, and supported my family and me. Were it not for them, I'm not sure how we would have fared. In spite of, or maybe because of these events, I look back with fondness on each place of ministry. Without hesitation, I affirm that what God accomplished in my family and the lives of many others was worth it all. As a family, we have said often, "If it took those things for us to be who we are now and to have what we now have, we'd do it all again and more without hesitation!"

Because of these life experiences, along with working through Scripture and reflecting often on God's Word, I have come up with a personal perspective on life in relationship to suffering from a biblical perspective. What follows is what I call my "Theology of Encouragement" to be worked out in succeeding chapters. This is my personal theology, which I have embraced over the course of decades.

> Every hurt, disappointment, and pain in life is placed there by a loving God who wills only the absolute best for His own, now and forever (Isa. 46:9–10; Ps. 84:11; Rom. 8:18, 31b–32, 37–39). God's goal is not so much ease and comfort in this life as it is His glory (Isa. 48:11) and the strength of His children's faith (Luke 22:31–32). God never allows anything into His children's life that is anything but good in His all wise knowledge (Rom. 8:28). God is so determined to make His children like His Son that He does not leave it to chance but wills it without any possibility of failure (Rom. 8:29). Therefore, everything the Christian experiences is ultimately good, increases joy, lays up treasure in heaven, and is to be understood in these contexts (Rom. 8:31–32).

In Scripture, the emotional life of the Christian is counterintuitive in that he or she is to rejoice while suffering as the norm rather than the exception. Thus, my personal theology has been most informed by a passage Paul wrote where a key phrase is, "Sorrowful, yet always rejoicing." I have taken this to mean that the Christian life isn't up or down, good or evil, blessing or suffering, or happy or sad. But rather, it's both up and down, good and evil, blessing and suffering, and happy and sad at the same time. Embracing the "both and" realities is essential to living the abundant life that Christ promised.[23] Paul describes a "both and" life in 2 Corinthians 6:4–10.

> As servants of God we commend ourselves in every way: by great endurance, in afflictions, hardships, calamities, beatings, imprisonments, riots, labors, sleepless nights, hunger; by purity, knowledge, patience, kindness, the Holy Spirit, genuine love; by truthful speech, and the power of God; with the weapons of righteousness for the

right hand and for the left; through honor and dishonor, through slander and praise. We are treated as impostors, and yet are true; as unknown, and yet well known; as dying, and behold, we live; as punished, and yet not killed; as sorrowful, yet always rejoicing; as poor, yet making many rich; as having nothing, yet possessing everything.

Through all "both and" events of life, I can confirm by experience that the Christian God is the God of comfort. Not only that, it is possible to dance in the dungeon of suffering joyfully for His glory. I pray that you will give serious consideration of these thoughts as they are worked out in the following chapters. Praise be to God, and to Him alone be all glory!

INTRODUCTION

· · · · · · · · · · · · · · · · · ·

What follows is not information for the brain, but Gospel medicine to strengthen the soul. Expect to meditate and think on the deep things of God. Prepare to be challenged by The Holy Spirit. Ready your soul to wrestle for God's blessing.[24] Your suffering is God's way of blessing you.

What is suffering? Dictionaries include the following definitions:[25] pain that is caused by injury, illness, loss, and so forth; or physical, mental, or emotional pain. Suffering is the condition of one who suffers; the bearing of pain or distress; the pain, misery, or loss experienced by a person who suffers; to experience or be subjected to something bad or unpleasant; or an experience of unpleasantness and aversion associated with the perception of harm or threat of harm in an individual. Suffering can be spiritual, emotional, psychological, physical, or all four together. The source can be a personal mistake, the actions of another, or natural calamity.

God uses suffering to get our attention and bring about His will. Through it, He builds our trust in Him and matures us in the faith when understood and processed biblically. Suffering is not necessarily virtuous, proof of holiness, or the way to gain God's favor. Suffering should be avoided unless doing so results in disobedience to God. It is God's will for His own to suffer for His glory and their spiritual maturity and to increase eternal rewards.[26]

Thus, I desire four things:

- For you to worship, honor, and glorify God when you suffer
- For you to have abiding joy when you experience difficult days
- For you to "dance" in your dungeon of adversity

- For you to share how God comforted you with others who struggle (2 Cor. 1:3–7).

The best way to assist you for those things is to describe the comforts by which God has comforted me.[27] I ask you to consider the process of how God comforted me as ways for Him to comfort you. God's comfort is not a pill you take one day and be healed the next. It is a regimen similar to chemotherapy for cancer patients or radical surgery to remove a tumor. Metaphorically, chemotherapy and surgery are God's Word.

Many cancer patients say chemotherapy almost killed them. Likewise, God's Word is so powerful at times that it is hard to embrace. But by accepting God's truth, no matter how difficult it is at the time, comfort and peace will always result.[28]

When the human body has invasive surgery, pain is involved, and yet it is required for physical healing. Why would we think anything less when God performs surgery on our soul? Scripture is sharper than any scalpel,[29] and God uses it to cut out the malignant tumors of doubt, fear, and lack of faith. Scripture is also the balm that heals the wounded and suffering.

God's Word is the surgeon's better scalpel. It is the oncologist's better chemotherapy. As Jesus prayed in John 17:17, "Sanctify them in the truth; your word is truth." God comforts His children through His Word. Thus, you will find many references to biblical texts in the following chapters because God's Word is living and active for your good. As often as you are able, access the scripture referenced in the endnotes for comfort and affirmation.

To experience God's comfort, delve deeply into the Bible. Immerse yourself in it. Set aside what people say about Scripture and believe the God of Scripture. Work through the hard passages by asking God to reveal His truth to you, and He will prove Himself to be the God of all comfort.[30] The comfort by which I have been comforted by God always came from Scripture.

I believe "the mind of Christ" is Scripture.[31] In Scripture, the Christian is given everything needed for life and godliness.[32] Above all things, *Dancing in the Dungeon* is how God used Scripture in the contexts of study, prayer, and worship to comfort me. I am strongly convinced that He will comfort you if you will seek to know Him better through His Word.

"Gold does not fear the fire."[33] After hearing those words from a friend and given the goal of *Dancing in the Dungeon*, I thought of 1 Peter 1:3–7.

> Blessed be the God and Father of our Lord Jesus Christ! According to his great mercy, he has caused us to be born again to a living hope through the resurrection of Jesus Christ from the dead, to an inheritance that is imperishable, undefiled, and unfading, kept in heaven for you, who by God's power are being guarded through faith for a salvation ready to be revealed in the last time. In this you rejoice, though now for a little while, if necessary, you have been grieved by various trials, so that the tested genuineness of your faith—more precious than gold that perishes though it is tested by fire—may be found to result in praise and glory and honor at the revelation of Jesus Christ.

My prayer is for those who read *Dancing in the Dungeon* is to not fear the fire of adversity. Gold may perish if the fire is intense enough, but a believer's faith never will because Jesus will not allow it.[34] I pray readers will have springs of living water welling up from within them[35] so they have joy and peace regardless of their life situations. I pray they will embrace that "every event of life is God calling (them) to a closer walk with Him."[36] Jesus said it this way, as recorded in Matthew 11:28–29, "Come to me, all who labor and are heavy laden, and I will give you rest. Take my yoke upon you, and learn from me, for I am gentle and lowly in heart, and you will find rest for your souls."

Chances are, you have been wounded. As a believer, you may have wanted to ask God, "Why?" but you were told you shouldn't question God. You may have wondered, "If God causes all things to work together for good, how is this good?" My goal is to affirm, "Just because we don't see how something can be good, it doesn't mean it isn't good,"[37] and, as a result, rejoice regardless of personal life events.

Many books have been written about suffering. This one is different. Rather than addressing the topic from a clinical approach or a series of Bible studies for theological reflection, *Dancing in the Dungeon* is written by one who has suffered and sought to understand God by asking "Why?" which led to comfort from God for peace, contentment, and joy.

The title for *Dancing in the Dungeon* comes from Acts 16:16–34, where Paul and Silas were beaten severely for preaching the gospel and then thrown in a dungeon with their feet shackled. It is written in verse 25, "About midnight Paul and Silas were praying and singing hymns to God." Emotionally and spiritually, they were dancing in the dungeon in spite of their physical wounds and geographical location.

The same happened to other apostles who suffered for their faith.[38] After being mobbed by a crowd and attacked by religious leaders, they were delivered miraculously.[39] Then they were arrested again with the intent to kill them,[40] but it was decided instead to beat them again and then release them.[41] Notice what is written about them in Acts 5:41, "They left the presence of the council, rejoicing that they were counted worthy to suffer dishonor for the name".

As a believer in Jesus Christ, you can dance in your dungeon of suffering. That is not a pipe dream. It is a promise from God who created the universe by speaking it into existence. It is backed by the promises of God who cannot lie and has been affirmed by believers for centuries. I add my affirmation regarding God's peace because I too have found Jehovah is the God of all comfort who comforts us in all our afflictions. Thus, the words of Jesus come to mind. "Come to me, all who labor and are heavy laden, and I will give you rest. Take my yoke upon you, and learn from me, for I am gentle and lowly in heart, and you will find rest for your souls. For my yoke is easy, and my burden is light" (Matt. 11:28–30).

And John 10:10 says, "I came that they may have life and have it abundantly." Finally, John 15:11 says, "These things I have spoken to you, that my joy may be in you, and that your joy may be full."

In keeping with these passages, consider what John Piper wrote on October 12, 2013, from his daily devotion app titled "Beware of Serving God":

> "The God who made the world and everything in it, being Lord of heaven and earth, does not live in temples made by man, nor is he served by human hands, as though he needed anything, since he himself gives to all mankind life and breath and everything" (Acts 17:24–25). We do not glorify God by providing His needs, but by praying that He would provide ours—and trusting Him to answer. Here we are at the heart of the good news of Christian Hedonism. God's insistence that we ask Him to give us help so that He gets glory (Ps. 50:15) forces on us the startling fact that we must beware of serving God and take special care to let Him serve us, lest we rob Him of His glory. This sounds very strange. Most of us think serving God is a totally positive thing; we have not considered that serving God may be an insult to Him. But meditation on the meaning of prayer demands this consideration. Acts 17:24–25 makes this plain. This is the same reasoning as in Robinson Crusoe's text on prayer: "If I were hungry, I would not tell you, for the world and its fullness are mine… Call upon me in the day of trouble; I will deliver you, and you shall glorify me" (Ps. 50:12, 15). Evidently, there is a way to serve God that would belittle Him as needy of our service. "The Son of Man came not to be served" (Mark 10:45). He aims to be the servant. He aims to get the glory as Giver.[42]

CHAPTER 1
WHAT GOD CAN DO

This book, and especially this chapter, is written for the reader to see how God comforted me in my hardships.[43] Then to consider his comfort for application in their situation. I present my life events, my faith, my belief, and my theology because, through these, God worked for my comfort. The most important element of God's comfort in my life has been embracing a biblical view of God.

I ask myself two questions in suffering (see the definition in the introduction) because the answers are comforting. What can God do? Anything. Why? Because He is God.

Ephesians 3:20 says, "Now to Him who is able to do far more abundantly than all that we ask or think, according to the power at work within us." Isaiah 46:9–10 says, "Remember the former things of old; for I am God, and there is no other; I am God, and there is none like me, declaring the end from the beginning and from ancient times things not yet done, saying, 'My counsel shall stand, and I will accomplish all my purpose.'" Finally, Ephesians 1:11 says, "[God] works all things after the counsel of His will."

The fact that God is able and will do far more abundantly than can be asked or imagined and works all things after the counsel of His will is profoundly encouraging. No matter what happens, God is able to handle it, turn it around, protect, and restore above what can be imagined. God is able to provide, help, and heal. God is able to do more things than can be imagined. The deeper the answer to "What can God do?" is driven into the heart, the more comfort and peace is experienced. The more often God's sovereignty is contemplated, the more contentment spreads through life. Meditating on Ephesians 3:20, Isaiah 46:9–10, and Ephesians 1:11 helps to wait on God and trust Him as He works His will in life in the midst of hard and difficult days.

To dance in the dungeon, the most important element is to embrace and understand God on His terms. In suffering, when everything is falling apart, the greatest comfort is knowing God will do His will for His glory and my ultimate good when and how He desires. Toward this end, my theology of encouragement is again presented as the end to which this chapter is aimed.

> Every hurt, disappointment, and pain in life is placed there by a loving God who wills only the absolute best for His own, now and forever.[44] God's goal is not so much ease and comfort in this life as it is His glory[45] and the strength of His children's faith.[46] God never allows anything into His children's lives that is anything but good in His all wise knowledge.[47] God is so determined to make His children like His Son that He does not leave it to chance but wills it without any possibility of failure.[48] Therefore, everything the Christian experiences is ultimately good, increases joy, lays up treasure in heaven, and is to be understood in these contexts.[49]

God is, always has been, and forever will be. He is perfect in everything He does. God does what glorifies Himself first and then whatever is ultimately good for His children, and the two never conflict.[50] God's own definition of love motivates Him. It's above the scrutiny of man, and it's bound only by His perfect nature. Everything God does is absolutely filled with perfect wisdom and love above man's ability to comprehend. God is God; no one else is. This is the foundation for understanding who God is, and I have found these truths are of essential importance to dance in the dungeon of adversity.

A friend once said to me, "There is a God who is and one you want Him to be. The two are not the same." Contemplating that statement caused me to consider who God says He is as found in Scripture. In His Word, God reveals himself clearly. Consider the following scriptures, read them slowly, and meditate long on who God is for your comfort while applying their meaning to your situation.

- "My thoughts are not your thoughts, neither are your ways my ways, declares the Lord. For as the heavens are higher than the earth, so are my ways higher than your ways and my thoughts than your thoughts" (Isa. 55:8–9).
- "His dominion is an everlasting dominion, and his kingdom endures from generation to generation; all the inhabitants of the earth are accounted as nothing, and he does according to His will among the host of heaven and among the inhabitants of the earth; and none can stay his hand or say to Him, 'What have you done?'" (Dan. 4:34–35).
- "See now that I, even I, am he, and there is no god beside me; I kill and I make alive; I wound and I heal; and there is none that can deliver out of my hand" (Deut. 32:39).
- "The Lord kills and brings to life; He brings down to Sheol and raises up. The Lord makes poor and makes rich; He brings low and he exalts. He raises up the poor from the dust; He lifts the needy from the ash heap to make them sit with princes and inherit a seat of honor. For the pillars of the earth are the Lord's, and on them he has set the world" (1 Sam. 2:6–8).
- "I am the Lord, and there is no other, besides me there is no God; I equip you, though you do not know me, that people may know, from the rising of the sun and from the west, that there is none besides me; I am the Lord, and there is no other. I form light and create darkness, I make

- well-being and create calamity, I am the Lord, who does all these things" (Isa. 45:5–7).
- "Thus says the Lord of hosts, the God of Israel, 'It is I who by my great power and my outstretched arm have made the earth, with the men and animals that are on the earth, and I give it to whomever it seems right to me'" (Jer. 27:4–6).
- "Our God is in the heavens; he does all that he pleases" (Ps. 115:3).
- "May the Lord direct your hearts to the love of God and to the steadfastness of Christ" (2 Thess. 3:5).

These passages set forth God's absolute sovereignty, power, and providence. There is nothing He cannot do. He proclaims His right to do whatever He chooses for His glory, and no one can question Him. This view of God has brought me great comfort many times and helped me trust Him absolutely. I find rest by believing who God is from His Word.

As a proof of what God can do, He once made a person do what he or she otherwise wouldn't have done without ever violating his or her will. This took place with the king of Assyria and the children of Israel, as found in Ezra 6:22. "And they [the Israelites] kept the Feast of Unleavened Bread seven days with joy, for the Lord had made them joyful and had turned the heart of the king of Assyria to them, so that he aided them in the work of the house of God, the God of Israel." Note a few phrases: "The Lord had made them joyful," "Had turned the heart of the king of Assyria to them," and "So that he [the king] aided them [Israelites]."

The Israelites' joy was the result of God's activity. "[He] made them joyful." God made them joyful by "[turning] the heart of the king of Assyria," as Proverbs 21:1 affirms, "The king's heart is a stream of water in the hand of the Lord; he turns it wherever he will." Because God turned the heart of the king of Assyria, "He [the king] aided them [Israelites] in the work of the house of God." And this was how God "made them [Israelites] joyful."

What can God do? Anything. Why? Because he's God. Can he make a person do something he or she otherwise wouldn't have done without violating his or her will? According to Ezra 6:22, He did, and He can do it again if and when He desires.[51] Because God can cause a person's heart to be changed without violating his or her will, which is a small thing for Him, is there anything He cannot do? Thus, can He handle the situation you are in? Christians should never doubt what God is able to do.

Doubting or questioning God's power improperly when in hard times is dangerous, as seen when Job questioned God and the Almighty's interrogation silenced him in Job 38:2–4.

> Then the Lord answered Job out of the whirlwind and said: "Who is this that darkens counsel by words without knowledge? Dress for action like a man; I will question you, and you make it known to me. Where were you when I laid the foundation of the earth? Tell me, if you have understanding."

After God put Job in his place by demanding replies to questions that Job couldn't answer, there is an interlude in Job 40:1–8. Consider God's questions of Job.

> And the Lord said to Job: "Shall a faultfinder contend with the Almighty? He who argues with God, let Him answer it." Then Job answered the Lord and said: "Behold, I am of small account; what shall I answer You? I lay my hand on my mouth. I have spoken once, and I will not answer; twice, but I will proceed no further." Then the Lord answered Job out of the whirlwind and said: "Dress for action like a man; I will question you, and you make it known to me. Will you even put me in the wrong? Will you condemn me that you may be in the right?"

Again, what can God do, and why can He do it? Paul may have reflected on this passage when he wrote in Romans 9:20–22, "Who are you, O man, to answer back to God? Will what is molded say to its molder, 'Why have you made me like this?' Has the potter no right over the clay, to make out of the same lump one vessel for honored use and another for dishonorable use?" Indeed, God is sovereign to work, do, and/or cause whatever He deems best. Amen!

> After God put Job in his place, Job gives a proper response in 42:1–2, 5–6.
>
> Then Job answered the Lord and said: "I know that you can do all things, and that no purpose of yours can be thwarted ... I had heard of you by the hearing of the ear, but now my eye sees you; therefore I despise myself, and repent in dust and ashes."

As has been said, the most important thing about us is what we believe about God. If we are to have a God who "is able to do exceeding and abundantly above all we ask or imagine,"[52] He must be sovereign, providential, omnipotent (all powerful), and omniscient (all knowing) unequivocally without exception or reservation. Then we will know He controls Satan to deliver us from any and all temptations and trials. If God is not absolutely sovereign, able to do whatever He so desires at anytime, anywhere, and with anyone, He is no longer God. If God is not all powerful to overrule mankind and providentially carry out His will in any, every, and all situations, then He is not God. It is impossible to have too high a view of God with a corresponding low view of man. This is the foundation for believing God is able to do exceeding and abundantly above all we ask or imagine.[53]

About Questioning God

When it comes to questioning God, everything hinges on attitude and expression of the heart. It seems when Job questioned God that his attitude may have been less than proper given the way God answered him. Once Job's attitude changed, his words also changed.[54] Now consider an event from John 11 when two sisters, Martha and Mary, both said the exact same thing to Jesus after their brother Lazarus died. Jesus confronted one sister while he comforted the other.

> When Martha heard that Jesus was coming, she went and met him, but Mary remained seated in the house. Martha said to Jesus, "Lord, if you had been here, my brother would not have died. But even now I know that whatever you ask from God, God will give you." Jesus said to her, "Your brother will rise again." Martha said to him, "I know that he will rise again in the resurrection on the last day." Jesus said to her, "I am the resurrection and the life. Whoever believes in me, though he die, yet shall he live, and everyone who lives and believes in me shall never die. Do you believe this?" ... When Mary came to where Jesus was and saw him, she fell at his feet, saying to him, "Lord, if you had been here, my brother would not have died." When Jesus saw her weeping, and the Jews who had come with her also weeping, he was deeply moved in his spirit and greatly troubled. And he said, "Where have you laid him?" They said to him, "Lord, come and see." Jesus wept. So the Jews said, "See how he loved him!" (John 11:20–26, 32–36).

In response to Martha's statement, Jesus gave her a theological lesson requiring a response. But when Mary made the exact same statement, Jesus was moved and wept without challenging her in any way. After reflecting on these two events, the conclusion I come to is that the sisters must have presented different attitudes to Jesus.

Because it is recorded Martha was probably a type A personality and Mary was more of a reflective person,[55] Jesus responded to them in the manner required given their temperament, heart, and attitude.

God does not mind being asked why or questioned as long as the attitude of the heart and presentation of the question are appropriate. Consider how Abraham interacted with God when, through prayer, he asked if God would destroy the righteous along with the wicked in Genesis 18:27–33. Abraham said to God, "What if I can find fifty righteous… Will you spare the city? What if I find forty… thirty… twenty… ten righteous, will you still destroy the city?" God allows Abraham to press Him, but notice Abraham's humble attitude toward God during the interchange.

- "I have undertaken to speak to the Lord, I who am but dust and ashes" (Gen. 18:27).
- "Oh let not the Lord be angry, and I will speak" (Gen. 18:30).
- "Oh let not the Lord be angry, and I will speak again but this once" (Gen. 18:32).

Consider it is recorded in Hebrews 4:16 how believers are told to "come boldly before the throne of grace to find help in time of need." Then there are numerous times in the book of Psalm that God is asked, "Why?"[56] When approaching God, attitude is everything. It is acceptable in your hurt and pain to go to the throne of grace seeking answers.[57] As it is written in James 1:5–6, "If any of you lacks wisdom, let Him ask God, who gives generously to all without reproach, and it will be given him. But let Him ask in faith, with no doubting." If God prohibited ever being asked "Why?" He would not have allowed Hebrews 4:16 or James 1:5–6 to be written, and He might have killed Abraham and Job for questioning him.

Embracing a Biblical View of God

With a biblical view of God, there is abundance of hope no matter what the situation is or may become. When the believer holds God in the highest of reverence and esteem, the Holy Spirit infuses peace and contentment in his or her heart regardless of circumstances. A solid biblical view of who God is will result in the believer joyfully affirming, "Though he slay me, I will hope in him" (Job 13:15).

> Though the fig tree should not blossom, nor fruit be on the vines, the produce of the olive fail and the fields yield no food, the flock be cut off from the fold and there be no herd in the stalls, yet I will rejoice in the Lord; I will take joy in the God of my salvation. God, the Lord, is my strength; He makes my feet like the deer's; He makes me tread on my high places (Hab. 3:17–19).

Either God is able, or He isn't. Those who study Scripture will conclude God is always good and loving—able to do anything anytime anywhere however he desires without needing to explain Himself or answer to anyone. They will conclude that God's wisdom in carrying out His will is always perfect and complete with everything He does being right. Consider what is written in Ephesians 1:11, "In (Christ) we have obtained an inheritance… who works all things according to the counsel of His will."

All things include all things. As Tim Keller said, "Just because we don't see how something can be good doesn't mean it isn't good." Contemplate that statement in light of God's interrogation with Job. Meditate on it in the context of God's omnipotence. Consider it in your life context. Those who think biblically on who God is will find profound comfort, peace, and rest. They will experience Jesus' promise from Matthew 11:28–30, "Come to me, all who labor and are heavy laden, and I will give you rest. Take my yoke upon you, and learn from me, for I am gentle and lowly in heart, and you will find rest for your souls. For my yoke is easy, and my burden is light."

In consideration of what God can do, reflect on Ephesians 3:20 phrase by phrase. Ask yourself, "What can God do?" Then emphasize each phrase in your mind, applying the scripture to your situation. By meditating on this passage, the Spirit will confirm that God is absolute in omnipotence and able to handle any situation you ever encounter. God is able to do far more abundantly than all we ask or think according to the power at work within us.

Because of these things and many more, believers can dance in the dungeon of personal adversity with peace, contentment, and joy. The rest of *Dancing in the Dungeon* works out having a God-centered attitude toward all of life's events and the God who is behind them all.[58] Because of these things, I believe my theology of encouragement tenaciously.

> Every hurt, disappointment, and pain in life is placed there by a loving God who wills only the absolute best for His own, now and forever. God's goal is not so much ease and comfort in this life as it is His glory and the strength of His children's faith. God never allows anything into His children's lives that is anything but good in His all wise knowledge. God is so determined to make His children like His Son that He does not leave it to chance but wills it without any possibility of failure. Therefore, everything the Christian experiences is ultimately good, increases joy, lays up treasure in heaven, and is to be understood in these contexts.

Discussion Questions

- Discuss why it is important to understand God on His terms from Scripture.
- What do you think about the author's theology of suffering?
- Discuss Jesus' responses to the statements from Mary and Martha in John 11:21 and 31 in terms of questioning God.
- Paraphrase and explain the meaning of Ephesians 3:20 in your own words.

Ron Ethridge Jr.

Reflection #1: God's Comfort in a Night from Hell

Enough time has passed since my "night from hell" took place that I can write about it. I relate this event because you may experience something similar. My hope is that, if or when you have a traumatic life event, you will flee to God, knowing He will most certainly comfort you.

Several years ago, I was awakened at 2:00 a.m. to my dad who was drunk and standing over his ninety-two-year-old bedridden mother yelling over and over, "Why don't you just damn die?!" The emotional shock and horror of that event still grieves me years later. I tried to get him to sit down, but he wouldn't. I tried to quiet him, but he cussed me. I tried everything I could think of to calm him down, but he only got worse. Finally, he passed out. I'll never forget my grandmother saying about her firstborn son, "It's okay. That's not him. It's the whisky talking." Only the love of a mother...

I couldn't go back to sleep. I had to get my grandmother out of that abusive situation and my dad into rehab. But how? I found out it is virtually impossible to admit someone into a nursing home unless he or she is already in a hospital. Then I was clueless how to get my dad into rehab against his will. For the first time in my life, I was at the proverbial end of my rope without a knot.

Mom was with me, and I told her I had to get away.[59] I went into a bedroom with my Bible, holding it like a teddy bear. For about forty-five minutes, I quoted every verse I could think of over and over. Some of the passages I prayed to God were:

- "There is therefore no condemnation for those who are in Christ Jesus."[60]
- "I can do all things through Christ who strengthens me."[61]
- "Delight yourselves in the Lord, and He will give you the desires of your heart."[62]
- "Trust in the Lord with all your heart and do not lean on your own understanding."[63]

- "God causes all things to work together for the good of those who love Him."[64]

Over and over, I cried out, "God, I need you. Reveal yourself to me. Come by my side. In Your Word, You said, 'Draw near, and you'll draw near to me. Please.' It is written, 'Let your requests be made known, and your peace will guard my heart and mind. Without you, I'm nothing. You are God. I trust you. I believe you. I love you. I praise you. You are my King and Savior!"

I passionately prayed Ephesians 3:20 numerous times. "God, you are able to do exceeding and abundantly above all that I ask or imagine, according to the power at work in me." I prayed these passages over and over. There were no requests or petitions because I was at a loss as to what to ask for.

Eventually, I came out exhausted and not feeling much better. Not long afterward, the phone rang. It was hospice. They had found a room for my grandmother, and she could move in that day. Then after making one other phone call, I was also able to get my dad into the hospital at the same time. God took care of both situations without me asking anything specific.

The point is that I didn't ask God for anything related to my grandmother or dad. He knew what I needed because the Spirit had been praying for me, my grandmother, and dad with groanings too deep for words.[65] All I did was seek God for who He is and nothing else. Thus, it is recorded Jesus said the following in Luke 12:28–31, "Do not seek what you are to eat and what you are to drink, nor be worried. For all the nations of the world seek after these things, and your Father knows that you need them. Instead, seek His kingdom, and these things will be added to you."

In a crisis, we need God Himself, not as a spiritual Santa Claus or divine 9-1-1, but the sovereign God of the universe who holds all things in His hand, the one "who is able to do exceeding and abundantly above all we ask or imagine." When you are stressed, go to God, seeking Him. Then be content with whatever He deems best for you, as found in Philippians 4:6–7. "Do not be anxious about anything, but in everything by prayer and supplication with thanksgiving let your requests be made known to God. And the peace of God, which surpasses all understanding, will guard your hearts and your minds in Christ Jesus."

Chapter 2

A THEOLOGY OF ENCOURAGEMENT

. . . .

To get the most out of this chapter, slow down as you read each Scripture passage with the following reflection. Apply each text to your personal situation. Ask God to reveal His truth. By doing these things I pray you will be strengthened and encouraged.

I have been blessed with a decent theological education,[66] but I was not directly taught how to understand or process suffering from a biblical perspective. I had to formulate a theology of suffering as life threw me curves I didn't expect. These conclusions did not come easy as often I wrestled with God as He used His Word to humble me. I struggled for hours as the Spirit corrected my thoughts, conforming my heart to His truth rather than what I wanted to believe. What is presented is the product of spiritual and emotional blood, sweat, and tears, which has resulted in great personal and spiritual encouragement.

My resources included Scripture, God's help to apply and understand His Word, messages on suffering by preachers I respect,[67] and the counsel of godly friends.[68] I pray these perspectives will be a starting point for you to formulate a biblical view of encouragement. Coming up with your own theology of encouragement is one of the most important things you can devote yourself to in your walk with God. Make sure your theology of encouragement is supported by Scripture by being careful not to form your theology and then finding scripture to support it.[69] The best practice is to read Scripture and ask God to conform your heart to His truth.

Timothy Keller writes in his book, *Walking with God through Pain and Suffering,*

> "One of the main ways a culture serves its members is by helping them face terrible evil and suffering... Sociologists and anthropologists have analyzed and compared the various ways that cultures train its members for grief, pain, and loss. And when this comparison is done, it is often noted that our own contemporary secular, Western culture is one of the weakest and worst in history at doing so."[70]

This evaluation is accurate, not only for American culture but also those who profess Christ. This should not be because the Christian faith is born out of adversity and suffering that Jesus' life, death, and resurrection overcomes.

> "Other cultures have seen day to day life as being filled with pleasures but behind it all is darkness or illusion. Christianity sees things differently. While other worldviews lead us to sit in the midst of life's joys, foreseeing the coming sorrows, Christianity empowers it's people to sit in the midst of this world's sorrows, tasting the coming joy."[71]

Of all people, Christians should be able to suffer joyfully in a manner that glorifies God. If they aren't able to do so, why? The answer must include that ministers are not adequately equipping God's people with the tools to prepare for and process suffering in a biblical manner.[72] Satan knows all he has to do to get believers off track in their faith is cause them hardship for many to become inactive while some will abandon God. However, Satan ignores that suffering will have the opposite effect of what he intends for genuine believers, their holiness, godliness, and conformity to Christ.[73]

For example, in one church, I delivered a series of messages on stewardship that included an exposition of Malachi 3:8–12. In the course of one message, I said, "I challenge you to test God as He offers in this text. Give faithfully for one year, and if you can honestly say at the end of that year that God has not blessed you, we will refund all you gave for the year."

Several months later, a young man died unexpectedly while recovering from drug abuse. His mom came to me after a morning worship service and said, "You said God would bless me if I would give faithfully. Well, I did and look what it got me!" She turned around and walked off, and I don't remember seeing her very often after that.

Even though I tried, her heart was understandably too wounded to grasp anything I said about God or suffering. I wondered if she would have processed her personal tragedy differently if I had been faithful to present a solid theology of suffering on a regular basis. From that point, I determined to make how to process, understand, and be prepared for suffering a regular part of my preaching and teaching ministry.

In the same congregation was a precious lady I'll call Joy. She was married to an abusive alcoholic while raising five stair-step children (each two years apart in age), walking them all to church every Sunday morning, evening, and Wednesday night. Once the children became adults, tragedies began. Joy told me about these events herself, some of which I witnessed. One child was murdered. Two more drank themselves to death. Another had problems Joy wouldn't define. Two weeks after one child passed, a grandchild committed suicide. Then her unbelieving husband got terminal cancer and refused to be saved.[74] Like many others, I wondered how much Joy could endure.

Through all those events, Joy never missed a worship service. Every time I saw her, she testified to how good God was. There was never a time anyone saw her that she didn't smile with a twinkle in her eye. Even when she was weeping in deep pain, she smiled and welcomed everyone. Joy never attended college or seminary and never served on a committee or taught Sunday school. When decisions had to be made, she wasn't consulted. Yet Joy was the person most admired in the congregation for strength of faith, prayer, and a daily walk with God. Satan threw an inordinate volley of grenades into her life, but he failed to shake her trust in and love of God. She had a good theology of encouragement.

E. M. Bounds has written, "The same sun that softens wax hardens clay."[75] One lady's loss resulted in anger and stumbling; another's resulted in greater love for God and a strong faith. From that point, I sought God's help to handle and process suffering so my heart would be more like my friend Joy. I also worked to help my brothers and sisters in Christ to be prepared for suffering when it came their way. I wanted to help God's people form a biblical theology of encouragement in suffering.

People like Joy occur when God accomplishes His work through the Holy Spirit applying Scripture in their hearts.[76] As part of this process, God causes the believer to have joy and rejoice in the midst of suffering.[77] Thus, it is impossible to overemphasize the importance of reading, understanding, and believing what God says about suffering. Only those who are intimately familiar with Scripture will be able to suffer joyfully in a manner that glorifies God. In John 17:15–20, Jesus emphasized the importance of Scripture in the lives of those he saves.

> I do not ask that you take them out of the world, but that you keep them from the evil one. They are not of the world, just as I am not of the world. Sanctify them in the truth; your word is truth. As you sent me into the world, so I have sent them into the world. And for their sake I consecrate myself, that they also may be sanctified in truth. I do not ask for these only, but also for those who will believe in me through their word.

The following passages of Scripture are what God has worked in me for comfort and encouragement by his Holy Spirit. I strongly implore you to meditate and reflect deeply on these passages in your copy of Scripture. Read the texts slowly several times. Ask God to reveal His truth and apply it in your life circumstances. Take God at His Word so Scripture drives your view of circumstances rather than circumstances determine your view of God.

After reading each text, consider my reflections while seeking God's truth for your life context. Over the years, God used these texts to form my theology of suffering. I pray the Spirit will comfort, encourage, and help you as much as He has me. The comments are written in the first person on purpose as they come from my personal experiences and reflection in difficulty.

- Genesis 50:20 says, "As for you, you meant evil against me, but God meant it for good."
  Personal Application: Every time you hear about that person saying or doing the things you think are harming you, keep Joseph's perspective in mind. What has, is, and will happen to you is nothing near what he dealt with over the course of seventeen years. If you will quit thinking the axis of the universe goes through your head and remember that God is in control, your life will become more stress free.[78] But every time you ignore Joseph's perspective, the result will be worry and anxiety. So which is better: peace, contentment, and rest or worry and anxiety?
- Psalm 119:67, 71 says, "Before I was afflicted I went astray, but now I keep your word. It is good for me that I was afflicted, that I might learn your statutes."
  Personal Application: Affliction is a hard thing to understand and difficult to go through. But here you are told it is a "good" thing. Personal guilt or innocence regarding affliction are irrelevant in the context of them being good because of the two things that result each time

you are afflicted. The thing to embrace is that, among the many purposes of God in suffering, these two are especially encouraging. It is proper to affirm that afflictions cause these two things in a way nothing else would.

- Psalm 84:11 says, "For the Lord God is a sun and shield; the Lord bestows favor and honor. No good thing does he withhold from those who walk uprightly [in Christ]."

  Personal Application: Do you believe God or doubt Him? Proof of God's love is the cross, not what happens to you. Because God is love[79] and good,[80] He is only capable of good toward you whether or not you see events as such. (You aren't omniscient.)[81] The way God chooses to bless you in His loving mercy will most certainly be done differently than you want or expect,[82] but it is perfect nonetheless. Because God gave his Son for you, there is nothing good He will keep from you.[83] Be encouraged!

- Proverbs 3:5 says, "Trust in the Lord with all your heart, and do not lean on your own understanding."

  Personal Application: If you trust in your ability or strength for deliverance, or anyone else's for that matter, you have forgotten God's command and will ultimately be disappointed. You aren't omniscient (all knowing) nor omnipotent (all powerful), so don't rely on yourself. Don't trust your emotions. They will lie to you and change like the wind. So purpose in your mind and heart to be encouraged by God's truth.

- Isaiah 46:9–10 says, "Remember the former things of old; for I am God, and there is no other; I am God, and there is none like me, declaring the end from the beginning and from ancient times things not yet done, saying, 'My counsel shall stand, and I will accomplish all my purpose.'"

  Personal Application: Listen to God. Reflect on what He proclaims about Himself. Then apply what He says to your situation, and let it dominate your mind rather than what your emotions tell you. Keep in mind that this passage is worked out in the context of God's love for you, which means everything that happens He has deemed as ultimately good for you[84] and no one can change it.[85] As you embrace God's words through Isaiah, you will be encouraged.

- Daniel 4:34–35 says, "All the inhabitants of the earth are accounted as nothing, and he does according to His will among the host of heaven and among the inhabitants of the earth; and none can stay his hand or say to him, 'What have you done?'"

    Personal Application: Do you wonder about the future? Keep in mind what God can do, especially that no person is able to stop or prevent whatever He wills. No one, not even you, can mess up your life to the point of God not using you for His glory. This is a strong word of encouragement.

- Habakkuk 3:16–19 says, "I hear, and my body trembles; my lips quiver at the sound; rottenness enters into my bones; my legs tremble beneath me. Yet I will quietly wait for the day of trouble to come upon people who invade us. Though the fig tree should not blossom, nor fruit be on the vines, the produce of the olive fail and the fields yield no food, the flock be cut off from the fold and there be no herd in the stalls, yet I will rejoice in the Lord; I will take joy in the God of my salvation. God, the Lord, is my strength; he makes my feet like the deer's."

    Personal Application: Now you will find out if you love God for His stuff or if you love Him. You've lost it. It's gone. There's nothing you can do to bring it back. You are upset, physically weak, and unable to sleep. Yet you're not in near the situation Habakkuk was. There was a very real probability that an invading army would kill him in the midst of complete economic collapse. Now, what is the worst thing that can happen? You could die, right? Big deal.

You go to heaven. Until you die, which will happen sooner than you think, choose to rejoice in God who saved you.
- Matthew 5:10–12 says, "Blessed are those who are persecuted for righteousness' sake, for theirs is the kingdom of heaven. Blessed are you when others revile you and persecute you and utter all kinds of evil against you falsely on my account. Rejoice and be glad, for your reward is great in heaven, for so they persecuted the prophets who were before you."

    Personal Application: Jesus proclaims that those who suffer for Him are blessed because they will inherit heaven. That means I must shift my perspective of understanding from what is happening now to the reality of what will be in eternity. I must believe God absolutely and take Him at His Word. As people are lying about my family and me, as they are disparaging our character, Jesus commands me to rejoice and be glad, which requires an act of my will based on His truth and not my perspective. I'm not to be a masochist who enjoys pain, but one who lives on delayed gratification promised by God who does not lie. So I choose to take the view that what my family and I are going through at the present puts us in good company[86] with those who've suffered for God before. There are people like Joseph in Genesis, David as he ran from Saul, Esther as she was uncertain about her future,[87] Isaiah, Jeremiah, John the Baptist,[88] Paul, and many untold millions who now are in heaven.[89]

- John 15:20 says, "Remember the word that I said to you: 'A servant is not greater than his master.' If they persecuted me, they will also persecute you."

    Personal Application: You have asked God to make you more like Jesus numerous times. Therefore, do not rebel against God and the means He uses to answer your prayer. Jesus warned that everyone who follows Him will be persecuted. So view the difficulties that are happening to you as an affirmation that you are a genuine follower of Christ. In this, you can rejoice because your name is written in heaven.[90]

- Romans 8:16–18 says, "The Spirit himself bears witness with our spirit that we are children of God, and if children, then heirs—heirs of God and fellow heirs with Christ, provided we suffer with Him in order that we may also be glorified with him. For I consider that the sufferings of this present time are not worth comparing with the glory that is to be revealed to us."

  Personal Application: There is a requirement/prerequisite to inheriting Christ, that is, being glorified with him and having the blessings of eternity, suffering. The Spirit affirms to my spirit that I am saved by allowing me to suffer for and because of Christ. There is no doubt that suffering will accompany all who are His true followers.[91] If I do not suffer because of Christ, I am not saved.[92] With this being the case, every time I have hardships associated with following Jesus, it is but another affirmation I am saved, so, this truth encourages me.

- The following passages say, "For those whom he foreknew he also predestined to be conformed to the image of his Son" (Rom. 8:29), "And I am sure of this, that he who began a good work in you will bring it to completion at the day of Jesus Christ" (Phil. 1:6), and "For it is God who works in you, both to will and to work for his good pleasure" (Phil. 2:13).

  Personal Application: God does not leave my sanctification, holiness, or conformity to Christ to chance. It will happen. This is clear when Paul writes Christians are "predestined to be conformed to the image of [Christ]."[93] Everything I can discern in Scripture and from those I trust is that God accomplishes "His good will" through adversity and difficulty. Therefore in this hardship and in those to follow,

I choose to understand what God is doing in the moment as ultimately good (as best I can with his help). Through every hardship, trial, and difficulty, God is making me more like Jesus, just as Christ said would happen.[94] God's good pleasure[95] (conformity to Christ) is a work He began and will be completed when I stand before Christ in eternity.[96]

- 2 Corinthians 1:3–7 says, "Blessed be the God and Father of our Lord Jesus Christ, the Father of mercies and God of all comfort, who comforts us in all our affliction, so that we may be able to comfort those who are in any affliction, with the comfort with which we ourselves are comforted by God. For as we share abundantly in Christ's sufferings, so through Christ we share abundantly in comfort too. If we are afflicted, it is for your comfort and salvation; and if we are comforted, it is for your comfort, which you experience when you patiently endure the same sufferings that we suffer. Our hope for you is unshaken, for we know that as you share in our sufferings, you will also share in our comfort."

Personal Application: The more I embrace the truths regarding God's purpose and will in my life to prepare me to stand before Him, the more I am comforted and encouraged by God from His Word when hard times settle into my life and family. God never allows anything to occur randomly. He always has a purpose for everything. Every event is based in His providential sovereignty for His glory and my ultimate good. In difficulty, this is a great and enduring comfort. The more I share in suffering with Christ, the more abundantly I will be comforted by God. And God's comfort is always sufficient when I have encountered difficulties of varying degrees. In fact, afflictions are designed for me to experience God's comfort and salvation. At the same time, my suffering and comfort from God has the effect of comforting others who suffer as I give testimony of God's comfort. The result of patiently enduring is a present and eternal hope in the God of comfort.

- 2 Corinthians 1:8–11 says, "For we do not want you to be ignorant, brothers, of the affliction we experienced in Asia. For we were so utterly burdened beyond our strength that we despaired of life itself. Indeed, we felt that we had received the sentence of death. But that was to make us rely not on ourselves but on God who raises the dead. He delivered us from such a deadly peril, and he will deliver us. On Him we have set our hope that he will deliver us again. You also must help us by prayer, so that many will give thanks on our behalf for the blessing granted us through the prayers of many."

    Personal Application: One of God's purposes for suffering, especially extreme suffering, is to teach a very important lesson, to make me rely on God and not myself or anyone else. When I find myself in the difficult of times, God is calling me to turn completely, totally, and absolutely without any reservation to Him and trust in Him alone. Unless a person can restore life to a four-day dead man,[97] he or she is not worthy of trusting in difficulty. Therefore, I will, by God's grace, keep turning to Him in prayer, worship, and reading Scripture. The manner in which I will turn to others is only for them to lift up prayer requests on my behalf to God.

- 2 Corinthians 4:7–12 says, "But we have this treasure in jars of clay, to show that the surpassing power belongs to God and not to us. We are afflicted in every way, but not crushed; perplexed, but not driven to despair; persecuted, but not forsaken; struck down, but not destroyed; always carrying in the body the death of Jesus, so that the life of Jesus may also be manifested in our bodies. For we who live are always being given over to death for Jesus' sake, so that the life of

Jesus also may be manifested in our mortal flesh. So death is at work in us, but life in you."

Personal Application: How many times must I be taught the same lesson that all power to help me in difficulties is from God? Then again, learning the lesson is preparation to trust God again because of what He has done in the past because of who He is. I may get knocked down, have black eyes, walk with a limp, and have all kinds of scars, but I am still here, being used by God for His glory. The more I suffer for Christ, the greater He is magnified in me and seen by others. And this is a good thing! I can expect this to continue for the rest of my life, unless the world's "comfort" is of more worth than God's power, love, and mercy, which it is not.

- 2 Corinthians 4:16–18 says, "So we do not lose heart. Though our outer nature is wasting away, our inner nature is being renewed day by day. For this slight momentary affliction is preparing for us an eternal weight of glory beyond all comparison, as we look not to the things that are seen but to the things that are unseen. For the things that are seen are transient, but the things that are unseen are eternal."

  Personal Application: All I can glean from God about suffering from Scripture keeps me from losing heart and giving up as God Himself strengthens me. My body and human nature are in various stages of breaking down and dying. However, God renews my spirit every day. Every time I turn to him, I am strengthened. The hardships I experience are nothing more than a gnat flying into my forehead. Suffering lasts about as long and feels about the same as that gnat when compared to spending eternity with God. Therefore, in the midst of suffering, it is good to focus my mind on God who is in heaven where I will soon be. I will have this perspective, God's grace, when life gets hard.

- 2 Corinthians 12:7 says, "To keep me from being too elated by the surpassing greatness of the revelations, a thorn was given me in the flesh, a messenger of Satan to harass me, to keep me from being too elated."
  Personal Application: God uses Satan's harassment and thorns as preemptive strikes to keep me from giving in to sin. God uses Satan to accomplish my sanctification. The hardship you are going through may actually not be corrective discipline from God; rather, it's His way of keeping you from venturing into rebellion had you not experienced this. Keep a Bible-centered perspective.
- Philippians 1:29 says, "It has been granted to you that for the sake of Christ you should not only believe in Him but also suffer for his sake."
  Personal Application: God has granted me these two things. I cannot have one without the other because they are both gifts from God. It is absolutely true that every person who receives a crown must first carry a cross.[98]
- Ephesians 3:20 (NIV) says, "Now to Him who is able to do immeasurably more than all we ask or imagine, according to his power that is at work within us."
  Personal Application: Okay, all this is a mess, so what can God do about it? You don't see any way out. You don't see how things can change. You don't think there is any hope. That just means you don't remember who God is. Read the verse again slowly. What do you think it would take for this situation to be turned around, healed, and rectified? Now, multiply that times ten thousand times ten thousand times ten thousand, and you have not begun to approach God's ability and power. What can God do? How big is your God? Look at verse 20 again. Where is His power at work? How can you not be anything but encouraged?
- 2 Timothy 3:12 says, "All who desire to live a godly life in Christ Jesus will be persecuted."

Personal Application: The hardship and struggle I am experiencing is because of choices I've made to live for Christ and follow God's call. This reality will accompany everyone who makes the same choices. Don't be so surprised as if something odd is happening or you don't "deserve" it.[99] If God gave you what was fair, you'd be in hell. God has not been fair to you. He has been merciful.

- Hebrews 12:4–14 says, "In your struggle against sin you have not yet resisted to the point of shedding your blood. And have you forgotten the exhortation that addresses you as sons? 'My son, do not regard lightly the discipline of the Lord, nor be weary when reproved by him. For the Lord disciplines the one he loves, and chastises every son whom he receives.' It is for discipline that you have to endure. God is treating you as sons. For what son is there whom his father does not discipline? If you are left without discipline, in which all have participated, then you are illegitimate children and not sons. Besides this, we have had earthly fathers who disciplined us and we respected them. Shall we not much more be subject to the Father of spirits and live? For they disciplined us for a short time as it seemed best to them, but he disciplines us for our good, that we may share his holiness. For the moment all discipline seems painful rather than pleasant, but later it yields the peaceful fruit of righteousness to those who have been trained by it. Therefore lift your drooping hands and strengthen your weak knees, and make straight paths for your feet, so that what is lame may not be put out of joint but rather be healed. Strive for peace with everyone, and for the holiness without which no one will see the Lord."

Personal Application: Because you are a Christian with a new nature and the old sin nature, you will constantly have to battle against sin. You need to shed blood to kill the old nature. God assists you in this by His loving discipline.

When God disciplines you (which feels like punishment), it is proof of his love. Always remember that! Also, your suffering (pain as a result of God's discipline) results in sharing his divine nature. While going through the process is painful, after God's purposes are accomplished, the result is peace I would not otherwise obtain. Therefore, endure with the assurance of what the outcome will be.

- 1 Peter 4:12–19 says, "Beloved, do not be surprised at the fiery trial when it comes upon you to test you, as though something strange were happening to you. But rejoice insofar as you share Christ's sufferings, that you may also rejoice and be glad when His glory is revealed. If you are insulted for the name of Christ, you are blessed, because the Spirit of glory and of God rests upon you. But let none of you suffer as a murderer or a thief or an evildoer or as a meddler. Yet if anyone suffers as a Christian, let Him not be ashamed, but let Him glorify God in that name. For it is time for judgment to begin at the household of God; and if it begins with us, what will be the outcome for those who do not obey the gospel of God? And 'If the righteous is scarcely saved, what will become of the ungodly and the sinner?' Therefore let those who suffer according to God's will entrust their souls to a faithful Creator while doing good."

Personal Application: Why are you so surprised and frustrated that this is happening to you? Instead of having a pity party, God would have you rejoice because this event is part of getting you ready for when Jesus returns so you will be glad. All the lies being told about you results in the opposite of what these people intend. God's glory rests on you. Think on that. Their insults meant to harm you actually result in more of God in your life. If that is the result, why not challenge them to bring it on? (On second thought, leave that in God's hands. To do otherwise would

- be giving them a stick to beat you with [v. 15]). Don't be ashamed by their lies, but rather give glory to God for what He is doing. Because suffering is God's will (v. 19), trust Him, and keep on honoring Him in your actions.[100]
- 1 Peter 5:6–10 says, "Humble yourselves, therefore, under the mighty hand of God so that at the proper time he may exalt you, casting all your anxieties on him, because he cares for you. Be sober-minded; be watchful. Your adversary the devil prowls around like a roaring lion, seeking someone to devour. Resist him, firm in your faith, knowing that the same kinds of suffering are being experienced by your brotherhood throughout the world. And after you have suffered a little while, the God of all grace, who has called you to his eternal glory in Christ, will himself restore, confirm, strengthen, and establish you."

  Personal Application: Yes, this is hard. No, it is not fair. What people are doing and saying are hurtful. Their words are wounding you, your family, and the bride of Christ. But do you believe God? Keep in mind what Pam said, "If we believe what we say we believe, how can we be angry with the ones God is using to make us more like Jesus?"[101] So trust God. His will is being done even though you can't see or understand it. Take all your hurts, fear, pain, and confusion to God in prayer. Throw it to Him like a fifty-yard bomb in football. Sure, Satan is part of the mix. Don't give in to him for a moment. After all, your Christian brothers and sisters aren't giving in. This hard thing will end. Then God will restore all your losses. He will confirm you are His. He will give you strength, and He will set your feet firmly on the foundation Jesus Christ laid down centuries ago. There is always hope for those in Christ.
- 1 John 3:19–20 says, "By this we shall know that we are of the truth and reassure our heart before him; for whenever

our heart condemns us, God is greater than our heart, and he knows everything."

Personal Application: Failure hurts. Mistakes are embarrassing. You failed because of mistakes. You don't want to see anyone or have him or her talk to you as a result. It's one thing for a few people to know you failed. It's another for hundreds to know and talk about it in a small town. It may not be your imagination that people whisper when they see you coming, but keep in mind that their opinion doesn't matter.[102] Neither your failure nor your mistake(s) have any effect on the love God has for you. He knows everything about you: all your secrets, everything no one else knows, all the sinful thoughts you've ever had, and every single solitary mistake you've ever made. And He still loves you. In spite of all the things you are guilty of, you are still forgiven. Your name is still written down in heaven. You are still one of His chosen ones. It is impossible for you to ever make a mistake so big, so huge, and so massive that God changes His attitude of love toward you. Not only that, it is impossible for you (or anyone else) to do anything that can keep God from both loving you and using you again for His glory. How big is your God? Rather than replaying your failures and mistakes in your mind, focus on the truth of God's love and experience His mighty comfort anew.

Final Thoughts

I have presented these reflections as a starting point for you to form your own theology of encouragement. As you reflect on Scripture,[103] seeking truth while asking God for revelation, He will comfort you and grant His peace that is beyond comprehension.[104]

Consider Elisabeth Elliot's theology of suffering and encouragement. Her husband, Jim, was one of four missionaries murdered by Auca warriors in Ecuador during the 1950s. The movie,

End of the Spear, depicts the story. In 1981, Mrs. Elliot wrote this about the event,

> The Auca story… has pointed to one thing: God is God. If he is God, he is worthy of my worship and my service. I will find rest nowhere but in His will, and that will is infinitely, immeasurably, unspeakably beyond my largest notions of what he is up to. God is the God of human history, and he is at work continuously, mysteriously, accomplishing his eternal purposes in us, through us, for us, and in spite of us… Cause and effect are in God's hands. Is it not the ___ of faith simply to let them rest there? God is God. I dethrone Him in my heart if I demand that he act in ways that satisfy my idea of justice… The One who laid the earth's foundations and settled its dimensions knows where the lines are drawn. He gives all the light we need for trust and obedience.[105]

Discussion Questions

- What are specific things and ways you have been taught to understand and handle suffering?
- What has been your observation and experience of the ways people process suffering?
- Has the way you have observed Christians process suffering been different? Explain.
- Explain how you agree or disagree with one or two of the Scripture reflections.

Reflection #2: Satan's Achilles Heel, Forgiveness

Only God can forgive and forget.[106] If you can forgive easily, you have not been wounded deeply.[107] Consequently, sometimes forgiveness is a process, not an event. Without going into detail, I am forgiving two people for their actions toward me from 1976.[108] Today in 2013, I think of them maybe once or twice a year, but for years, the struggle was hard as I worked often to forgive them. Even while writing this, I am having to go back through the process of forgiving them again, and I'm glad. Let me explain.

My willingness and ability to forgive is one proof I've been forgiven.[109] If I will not forgive, it implies I have not been forgiven.[110] Because God (through Jesus) has forgiven me of transgressions that far surpass anything anyone has or can do to me, how can I do anything but forgive others? Forgiveness is God's chosen means by which restoration and reconciliation take place. Forgiveness is the language of heaven, and I want to speak it often. Every time I am called to forgive, I am reminded that God has forgiven me, so I can forgive.

Then there is the element of ongoing forgiveness I have learned to enjoy. When I must go through the process of continuing to forgive, I talk at the adversary. I do this because I want him or her to hear and be reminded of Jesus' death and resurrection and the fact I have been forgiven and my name is written in heaven. I want him or her to experience failure again. So when hurts tempt me to become bitter and unforgiving, I say the following out loud,

> Listen, Satan. Because I've been forgiven by God through Jesus, my name is written down in heaven. There is therefore no condemnation for me because I am in Christ Jesus, and there is nothing you can do about it. It is impossible for you to separate me from the love of God. Because Jesus has forgiven me, I am able and will continue to forgive this person. If you remind me of how he or she wounded me every hour, you will hear

me forgive him or her every hour. Every time you bring this person to my mind, you will hear me forgive him or her. The more often you remind me of him or her and what he or she did, the more I will be reminded to ask God to bless him or her and reveal Himself to him or her. As often as you want to be reminded of Jesus' power through his resurrection, feel free to remind me about that person and what he or she did.

I have found myself comforted and strengthened when I keep on forgiving in this manner as Jesus commands.[111] James was right when he wrote in James 4:7–8, "Submit yourselves therefore to God. Resist the devil, and he will flee from you. Draw near to God, and he will draw near to you." I have found praying in this manner is a wonderful way to apply James 4 and the process of forgiving. May God give you the same peace and joy by forgiving others. Remember that Satan's Achilles heel is forgiveness!

Chapter 3

HEAVEN... THE BEST IS YET TO COME

As mentioned previously, each chapter presents the comforts God has worked in me when I have struggled so as to comfort others with the comfort by which I have been comforted by God.[112] What follows is a powerful, regular, significant, and encouraging comfort I rely on from Him. Consider Paul from Colossians 3:1–4. Meditate on his words at length before proceeding further.

Seek the things that are above, where Christ is, seated at the right hand of God. Set your minds on things that are above, not on things that are on earth. For you have died, and your life is hidden with Christ in God. When Christ who is your life appears, then you also will appear with Him in glory.[113]

What will heaven be like? I don't know in my wildest imagination, but it will be more than I can imagine.[114] So, I like to imagine what heaven might be like. Some thoughts are certain; some I hope for. You would do well to follow Paul's encouragement and contemplate what heaven will be like, too.

There have been times when my struggles were so heavy that they drove me to wish this life was over.[115] I have longed to hear an angelic trumpet resound, knowing it means Jesus is back.[116] I have wanted to hear the shout of an angel from heaven proclaiming, "Come up here."[117] I have desired to be walking by a cemetery and see saints being resurrected and ascending to heaven, knowing the rapture is next.[118] The thought of what it would be like to not die[119] but be changed from mortal to immortal and be caught up to meet Christ in the air[120] is beyond my ability to comprehend. I have dreamed about what it will be like the first time I get to see Jesus with my own eyes. I can't count the times I've looked to the east early in the morning, trying to envision the clouds being rolled back as a scroll and Jesus returning in triumphant glory.[121] For these reasons and many more, I love to think and sing about heaven. I long to be with Christ because this life will then be nothing more than a bad dream quickly forgotten.

When hardship, pain, and difficulty come into my life, I rest in the sure knowledge that shortly I will die and stand before God.[122] Soon, God will send an angel to usher me into His presence.[123] Or I will not die but be changed in the twinkling of an eye from flesh to spiritual.[124] Either way, I will join in Jesus' triumphant return to earth.[125] As I enter God's presence for the first time, He will rejoice.[126] Words cannot explain or express the joy of what it will be like to see Jesus standing with a smile and open arms welcoming me home.

The redeemed of all time fill heaven. Only members of God's family will be there.[127] All present will know perfect comfort, love, joy, and peace.[128] Moses, Paul, Abraham, Joseph, David, and all the saints call everyone else by name because there are no strangers there. Every moment is one huge family reunion where everyone rejoices to see each other.

There won't be any babies crawling in heaven, which means my brother Lloyd who died before turning one day old will be an adult as we talk and get to know each other. My granny won't have hearing aids, glasses, or a walker. She will be in perfect health. I will finally meet the child my wife and I never saw who spontaneously aborted before taking a single breath. The child will be an adult like my little brother.

We will all celebrate and worship Jesus together. I like to think that, in heaven, everyone is about thirty-three years old in human terms, but perfect in every way like Adam and Eve were before the fall, as Jesus was in the resurrection.[129] No one will be blind, deaf, fat or skinny, crippled, or mentally challenged. No one will be physically, emotionally, psychologically, or spiritually imperfect in any way, shape, form or fashion. In heaven, everyone has love for everyone else, being both perfect and sinless because of the redeeming blood of Jesus Christ. Praise be to God!

For all eternity, everything will get better and better, newer and newer, sweeter and sweeter, nicer and nicer, and more perfect. Eyesight will get sharper, hearing will become more acute, the nuances of taste will improve, and the mind will comprehend ever-increasing complexities, mysteries, and truths. Through eternity, believers will become more and more and more perfect. This is what Jesus meant when He said what is recorded in Revelation 21:5, "Behold, I am making all things new(er) and newer and newer and newer..." (my paraphrase). This is like being given your dream car, and from that moment, free high octane gasoline stays filled in the gas tank. The paint shines brighter, the tires grip the road better, the engine's MPG keeps improving, the windows get clearer, and the new car smell gets sweeter. And all these things keep on improving for eternity. It's an insufficient illustration, but it's the best I can think of.

Then there are other minor things about heaven. Every believer has his or her own house, room, or mansion, tailored specifically and exactly by Jesus to be perfect for them.[130] Angels may serve believers (our guardian angel from Matt. 18:10). God's light shines everywhere so there are no shadows or night.[131] The fruit of the Tree of Life is available for healing the nations.[132] The streets are pure gold and clear as glass.[133] There are twelve gates, each one a single pearl,[134] that never closes because there are no enemies to fear. Nothing accursed will exist. Worship in the presence of God is continual.[135] A river of living water flows from God's throne.[136] Above all these things is God sitting on his throne. And Christians will reign with God forever! Thus what is written in Revelation 22:1–5,

Then the angel showed me the river of the water of life, bright as crystal, flowing from the throne of God and of the Lamb through the middle of the street of the city; also, on either side of the river, the tree of life with its twelve kinds of fruit, yielding its fruit each month. The leaves of the tree were for the healing of the nations. No longer will there be anything accursed, but the throne of God and of the Lamb will be in it, and his servants will worship him. They will see his face, and his name will be on their foreheads. And night will be no more. They will need no light of lamp or sun, for the Lord God will be their light, and they will reign forever and ever.

Every believer is given a crown and a special name that no one else has.[137] When the Book of Life is opened, the new name, rather than earthly names, are called out. When this unique name is called, only the person to whom it has been given can answer "Here!" and he or she will be deemed as one of Jesus' sheep to enter heaven. There will be no confusion about who is and isn't allowed into God's presence. No sinner or evil person will be with the redeemed in glory.[138]

Entertainment? In heaven? Of course because it will glorify God. Because the Spirit vested music with great power to move the soul in worship of Him, there will be music in heaven. By comparison, the most wonderfully magnificent opus Bach ever wrote is but banging of sticks compared to what will be heard in glory. I've wondered what a ten thousand-piece orchestra backed up by a million-voice angelic choir singing thousand-part harmony sounds like. If the music of a fallen sinner, with words written by another sinner, can lift a heart in praise and adoration of God,[139] what will it be like in heaven when perfect music and words will be heard in God's presence? Maranatha![140]

Then the most awe-inspiring and amazing thing of all eternity will happen at the marriage feast of the Lamb. The Lord Jesus Himself will serve believers.[141] Jesus Christ, the Great I Am, the creator of the universe, will serve those redeemed from the curse of sin. Imagine if possible, the second person of the Trinity will serve all the redeemed of all eternity in glory. This is described by Jesus in Luke 12:35–37,

> Stay dressed for action and keep your lamps burning, and be like men who are waiting for their master to come home from the wedding feast, so that they may open the door to Him at once when he comes and knocks. Blessed are those servants whom the master finds awake when he comes. Truly, I say to you, he will dress himself for service and have them recline at table, and he will come and serve them.

The joy, shock, and awe of that event may be much like Peter had when Jesus washed his feet in John 13:3–11. This event will so overwhelm the participants that the only proper response will be what is recorded in Revelation 4:9–11, casting crowns to Jesus' feet in worship of Him. Then all of creation, along with all the redeemed and all the angels, will worship saying, "Holy, holy, holy is the Lord God Almighty!"[142]

Who can call to mind what the marriage feast of the Lamb will be like? What kind of food will be set before us? What kind of drink? How many courses? Who will we sit beside, and what will be his or her story of salvation? What will the angels be doing? What will the banquet room look like? How long will the feast last? What will dessert be? There won't be any need to worry about gaining weight by eating too much. All these questions and more flood my mind as I look forward to one day being in heaven with God the Father, God the Son, and God the Holy Spirit.

Imagine the following:

- Adam and Eve describing the garden of Eden before the fall
- Joseph giving the details of his life only briefly described in Scripture about being sold into slavery, being falsely accused of rape, serving in prison, being elevated to vice pharaoh, and then seeing his brothers again

- Moses recounting events not found in Scripture and going into detail about the plagues, the exodus, crossing the Red Sea, receiving the Ten Commandments, and wandering in the wilderness
- David explaining in greater detail all the stories found in the Bible about him as he plays a harp and sings psalms he wrote
- Apostles telling their stories of being with Jesus for three years, seeing Him after the resurrection, and describing what their lives were like after Pentecost
- Elijah and Elisha describing seeing the chariots of fire

Then time prevents describing conversations with other great saints: Clement, Polycarp of Smyrna, John Chrysostom, Augustine, Martin Luther, John Calvin, William Carey, Justin Martyr, David Brainerd, Jonathan Edwards, and Charles Haddon Spurgeon, not to mention all the other nameless saints over the millennia that are highly regarded in heaven.

I wonder if we will be given a visual presentation of the six days of creation. Will we watch the flood take place and see the first rainbow? Will we have all or any our questions answered? How many times will we get to see the resurrection, Pentecost, and ascension played back? How long will we get to have personal one-on-one time with the Trinity? What will our assignments be as we reign with God for eternity?[143]

Will the Holy Spirit explain scriptures we've always wondered about, explaining the eternal meaning of each book, chapter, paragraph, sentence, and word of Scripture? How awesome it will be to have the deepest truths of Scripture revealed by God Himself! Imagine sitting down with the author of each Bible book as he relates the process of writing. Visualize listening to Isaiah describe in detail the visions associated with writing the book bearing his name and then the same thing with Jeremiah, Moses, Amos, Jonah, Habakkuk, Mark, Matthew, Paul, and all the other biblical authors.

And then there is what makes heaven what it is, heaven, God's presence. Finally, the one who loved us perfectly will no longer be seen by faith, but we will be face-to-face. The wait to see Him will be over. Seeing, hearing, and touching Him will bring so much joy, peace, and contentment. All the questions we thought we'd ask will be forgotten. Kneeling before Jesus will so captivate the soul. Catching up with family and friends won't matter for ten million years because there's plenty of time for those minor desires later. God's presence will infuse everyone with absolutely perfect overwhelming love, happiness, joy, contentment, and peace that can only be experienced on earth in the most miniscule way.

Take everything else together (family, crowns, streets of gold, food, peace, and so forth), it is no longer heaven without God's presence. The joy and blessing of heaven is being in the presence of God the Father, God the Son, and God the Holy Spirit forever in perfect love, harmony, and acceptance.

Then, after billions of years spent worshipping God with all the redeemed of all ages, there is time to spend tens of thousands of years with each brother and sister in Christ individually. Thousands of years talking one-on-one with Adam, Eve, Enoch, Mary, Moses, Hannah, David, Samuel, Esther, Job, Solomon, Paul, John, Isaiah, Samson, Habakkuk, Peter, Barnabas, the thief on the cross, and Naomi with them being as interested in listening to our stories as telling their own.

For all these reasons, I like to sing songs about heaven to get my heart ready for when I am there one day. Every time I contemplate what soon will be, this life becomes less important. All the things I worry about fade into obscurity. My troubles lose their significance. And I find myself looking toward heaven rather than what happens around me or to me. That is just one fallen human's dim view of what heaven might be like that falls short of what heaven will actually be.

Oh, think long and often about heaven! Follow Paul's encouragement from Colossians 3:1–4.

> Seek the things that are above, where Christ is, seated at the right hand of God. Set your minds on things that are above, not on things that are on earth. For you have died, and your life is hidden with Christ in God. When Christ who is your life appears, then you also will appear with Him in glory.

Discussion Questions

- Why or why not would you agree with "to be of earthly good the Christian must be heavenly minded"?
- What do you think of the author's projections about what heaven may be like?
- Describe what you think heaven may include that the author does not address.

Dancing in the Dungeon

Reflection #3: Whether in Waves or Caves, Be Faithful

It seems like some Christians receive many blessings while others have heartbreaks one after another. This reflection is a potential answer to that mystery. During a recent time of difficulty, I was reading Scripture, asking God to reveal Himself.[144] I eventually came to Hebrews 11, affectionately known to many as "the Hall of Faith." Because I had read and taught the passage before, I went on autopilot as I read the chapter.

I was familiar with all those mentioned: Able, Enoch, Noah, Abraham, Isaac and Jacob, and Sarah. I was familiar with the words that described them, "These all died in faith, not having received the things promised, but having seen them and greeted them from afar" (11:13). Nothing new. Nothing struck me as fresh so I continued reading.

Moses, the children of Israel, and Rahab the prostitute were commended for their faith. Then in 11:32–35, the writer recounts others in quick succession he didn't have the time to expand upon.

> Gideon, Barak, Samson, Jephthah, of David and Samuel and the prophets—who through faith conquered kingdoms, enforced justice, obtained promises, stopped the mouths of lions, quenched the power of fire, escaped the edge of the sword, were made strong out of weakness, became mighty in war, put foreign armies to flight. Women received back their dead by resurrection.

From 11:3–35, people were described of whom it could be said they rode the wave of God's blessing. Then halfway through 11:35, the author turns on a dime. Instead of describing those who rode the wave, he described those on the other end of the spectrum by recounting lives of extreme suffering. From 11:35–B to 11:38, the following is written,

> Some were tortured, refusing to accept release, so that they might rise again to a better life. Others suffered mocking and flogging, and even chains and imprisonment. They were stoned, they were sawn in two, they were killed with the sword. They went about in skins of sheep and goats, destitute, afflicted, mistreated—of whom the world was not worthy—wandering about in deserts and mountains, and in dens and caves of the earth.

I should have noticed the contrast before, but I never had. This was new. In addition to those who rode the wave of God's blessing, some lived in caves_with persecutions. Of this group, those who suffered and chose to suffer, these are the ones of whom it is written, "The world is not worthy." Then came the lynchpin in 11:39–40, "And all these, though commended through their faith, did not receive what was promised, since God had provided something better for us, that apart from us they should not be made perfect."

"And all these." Both those who rode the wave of God's blessing and those who lived in caves are in God's Hall of Faith. Those who experienced the highs of serving God and those who suffered are in the Hall of Faith. Being in this highly honored group is not dependent on success in terms that the world assigns. Which subgroup of the one group a Christian is in is not of his or her choosing, but rather God's providence.[145] He determines who rides a wave or lives in a cave. If He so chooses, He can move whoever He desires from the wave to a cave or from the cave to the wave because He is the one "who works all things after the counsel of His will."[146]

Those who ride the wave of God's blessing should humbly thank God for their position. They should love and pray for those in caves. They should never say to those in caves that, if they "did things better," "worked harder," or "had more faith," they would ride the wave like they do. That would be prideful and improper for God's servants.

Likewise, those in a cave should praise God for blessing those riding the wave. The call on their lives and how it is manifested is as important and significant as any other servant in God's economy.

They should be careful not to resent them, but be faithful in whatever situation they find themselves in.

Whether a servant of God is riding the wave or living in a cave, they are in the Hall of Faith. What determines their place in God's hall is faithfulness to his call, not where they carry out God's call. Whether Christians ride waves or live in caves, they are to be faithful.[147]

If your life seems to be spent more in caves than riding waves, know that God placed you there to honor Him by being faithful. You are not in a cave as punishment or because you failed. You are there because God deemed it good for you to serve Him there, and one day, you will hear Him say, "Well done, good and faithful servant. You have been faithful over a little; I will set you over much. Enter into the joy of your master."[148]

Chapter 4

WHY ME, WHY THIS, WHY NOW

Because God is the same yesterday, today, and forever,[149] what Paul wrote about God's work in Him is also possible for God to do in us. Consider what is recorded in Philippians 4:11–13,

> Not that I am speaking of being in need, for I have learned in whatever situation I am to be content. I know how to be brought low, and I know how to abound. In any and every circumstance, I have learned the secret of facing plenty and hunger, abundance and need. I can do all things through Him who strengthens me.

Because there is nothing God cannot do,[150] there is no reason to doubt God has, can, and will work the same contentment in believers today as found in Philippians 4:11–13.[151] The way this is accomplished by the Spirit is as we "hide His Words in our heart so that we will not sin against him."[152] Thus, the purpose of this chapter is to present passages of hope for reflection, encouragement, and comfort.

Paul asks a question worthy of us asking in Galatians 3:4, "Did you suffer so many things in vain?" The implication is that suffering multiple ways over time is intended by God to have specific results. Depending on your view of God, understanding of Scripture, and the way those things affect how you process life, you will either look for and find reasons to grow in Christ, or you will be a fatalist living without hope or purpose in life. The fatalist believes whatever is going to happen will happen. Those who believe in God's providence know everything happens with a purpose and reason willed by the all good, loving, and wise heavenly Father. My prayer is that you will process your life events through the sieve of Bible truth. I pray God will help you redeem your hardships for His glory and your comfort.

Meditating on God through Scripture is one way He comforts those in affliction. I have found it helpful to often return to God's Word and meditate on His truths to refocus my heart on God's reality rather than my assumed false omniscience. This chapter is designed to present a truth, briefly comment on it, and provide supporting scripture. There are many ways to apply what follows. The important thing is to drive the truth of God's Word deep into your spirit for the Spirit to comfort you. These thoughts are written in the first person when I asked, "God, why is this happening?" The foundation begins with James 1:2–4 where it is written, "Count it all joy, my brothers, when you meet trials of various kinds, for you know that the testing of your faith produces steadfastness. And let steadfastness have its full effect, that you may be perfect and complete, lacking in nothing."

It is easy to agree intellectually with James, but it's hard to be joyful when hurting unless the reasons to "count it all joy" are embraced. Joy isn't because of the trial but rather what God is accomplishing through the trial. Thus, God gave me the following reflections to "count it all joy" when suffering. These are in no specific order after the first two.

God's Glory

The single-most important thing in the universe is God's glory. The fact is that God will glorify His name in all things, including His children's suffering. His glory is more important to Him than your personal ease, comfort, or temporal blessings. Only when God's glory is more important than anything else can one count it all joy when suffering. Consider the following:

- "For my own name's sake I delay my wrath; for the sake of my praise I hold it back from you, so as not to cut you off. See, I have refined you, though not as silver; I have tested you in the furnace of affliction. For my own sake, for my own sake, I do this. How can I let myself be defamed? I will not yield my glory to another" (Isa. 48:9–11).
- "All this is for your benefit, so that the grace that is reaching more and more people may cause thanksgiving to overflow to the glory of God" (2 Cor. 4:15).
- "Jesus said this to indicate the kind of death by which Peter would glorify God" (John 21:19).
- "Now is my soul troubled. And what shall I say? 'Father, save me from this hour'? But for this purpose I have come to this hour. Father, glorify your name. Then a voice came from heaven: 'I have glorified it, and I will glorify it again'" (John 12:27–28).

Suffering Is God's Will

God's will and glory are above, beyond, and more significant than anything I can want or desire. God's will is to bless through suffering. While every Christian wants to be in God's will, most don't understand His will is for him or her to suffer as His way of blessing him or her. As it is written:

- "Jesus said, 'Truly, I say to you, there is no one who has left house or brothers or sisters or mother or father or children or lands, for my sake and for the gospel, who will not receive a hundredfold now in this time, houses and brothers and sisters and mothers and children and lands, with persecutions, and in the age to come eternal life'" (Mark 10:29–30).
- "Remember the word that I said to you: 'A servant is not greater than his master.' If they persecuted me, they will also persecute you" (John 15:20).

- "For it has been granted to you that for the sake of Christ you should not only believe in Him but also suffer for his sake" (Phil. 1:29).
- "All who desire to live a godly life in Christ Jesus will be persecuted" (2 Tim. 3:12).
- "The Spirit himself bears witness with our spirit that we are children of God, and if children, then heirs—heirs of God and fellow heirs with Christ, provided we suffer with Him in order that we may also be glorified with him" (Rom. 8:16–17).

Through Suffering, Humility Is Accomplished

An enemy within me is pride, also known as selfishness and self-centeredness. It is impossible to be conformed to the image of Christ as long as pride is present in my heart. Thus, God works to eliminate a prideful attitude that opposes humility. A powerful example of God attacking pride is the preemptive strike that God took in Paul's life, which is representative of what He does in all His children. By knowing God is accomplishing humility through hardship, there is reason to count it all joy.

> To keep me from becoming conceited because of these surpassingly great revelations, there was given me a thorn in my flesh, a messenger of Satan, to torment me. Three times I pleaded with the Lord to take it away from me. But he said to me, "My grace is sufficient for you, for my power is made perfect in weakness." Therefore I will boast all the more gladly about my weaknesses, so that Christ's power may rest on me. That is why, for Christ's sake, I delight in weaknesses, in insults, in hardships, in persecutions, in difficulties. For when I am weak, then I am strong (2 Cor. 12:7–10).

Suffering Reveals the Need for Sanctification

I do not know what is needed to become more like Jesus, primarily because of personal blind spots. By definition, I am not able to see my blind spots. The danger of a blind spot is that pride and conceit can slowly creep into the heart.[153] Thus, God works through suffering to reveal my blind spots to me. Because of his blind spot, Paul was unaware of his need for sanctification in the area of pride until the messenger of Satan was sent into his life. Only then did he understand the thorn of suffering as a blessing from God. In suffering, I see for myself what God knows (and works to correct) through the thorns of suffering. And therein is a reason to count it all joy (2 Cor. 12:7–10).

Suffering Teaches Complete Rest in God's Power

Everyone has a breaking point. Sooner or later, everyone can be pushed to the end of his or her rope. Sometimes God purposely puts me in difficulty to remind me who is able (Him) and who isn't (all others).[154] Those who are wise learn to trust God in good and bad times knowing He controls them all.[155] Those who walk with God delight in their weaknesses because then He is glorified as they rely on Him alone. Thus, it's a reason for joy (2 Cor. 12:7–10).

Suffering Is God's Method of Sanctification

Knowing what God is doing, glorifying His name, doing His will, humbling His servant, revealing the need for sanctification, and causing complete rest in his power means being more conscious of the big picture of God's work in me. Being conscious of God making me more like Jesus is a blessing Job didn't have. Thus, there is joy by knowing God is in the process of sanctifying me and making me more like Jesus (Job 1–2).

Suffering Conforms to Christ's Image

God is so determined to make me more like his Son th[at he] does not leave it to chance. There is no possibility whatsoever that I will not become more like Jesus because God predestines both the process and result. There is no possibility of God failing what He wills to accomplish. There is no possibility of any Christian not becoming more holy, more godly, and more like Jesus. This is a wonderful reason to count it all joy when suffering. "For those whom He foreknew He also predestined to be conformed to the image of his Son" (Rom. 8:29).

Suffering Draws Believers Closer to God

The same sun that softens wax hardens clay. When dark days invade my life, I have found my heart drawn to God. Whatever draws me closer to God and makes me more like Jesus is worth it. As is found in the hymn, "A Mighty Fortress Is Our God," "Let goods and kindred go, this mortal life also; The body they may kill: God's truth abideth still, His kingdom is forever." "Before I was afflicted I went astray, but now I keep your word. It is good for me that I was afflicted, that I might learn your statutes" (Ps. 119:67, 71).

Jesus Is Manifested

Because of Christ in me, I am able to suffer in a manner that glorifies God. As a result, the more I am filled with the Spirit, the more others see Jesus in me. As God comforts and sustains me in hard and difficult times, the resurrection power of Jesus is manifested to the world, and as a result, God is glorified. Thus, it's a reason to count it all joy.

> But we have this treasure in jars of clay, to show that the surpassing power belongs to God and not to us. We are afflicted in every way, but not crushed; perplexed,

> but not driven to despair; persecuted, but not forsaken; struck down, but not destroyed; always carrying in the body the death of Jesus, so that the life of Jesus may also be manifested in our bodies. For we who live are always being given over to death for Jesus' sake, so that the life of Jesus also may be manifested in our mortal flesh. So death is at work in us, but life in you (2 Cor. 4:7–12).

Suffering Results in Spiritual Maturity

The biblical attitude toward suffering is found in embracing what God is doing in an event and participating in what He is doing, specifically growing in Christ likeness. Joy is not in the trial, but rather, it's the eventual result and outcome the trial will produce, conformity to Jesus. Thus, it's a powerful reason to count it all joy.

> Count it all joy, my brothers, when you meet trials of various kinds, for you know that the testing of your faith produces steadfastness. And let steadfastness have its full effect, that you may be perfect and complete, lacking in nothing (James 1:2–4).

Suffering Results in Sharing Christ's Glory

Because suffering is God's will to sanctify and conform me to the image of Christ, I will not be surprised when hard times enter my life because God has ordained them for His glory.[156] I'm rejoicing because sharing in Christ's sufferings also means sharing in His glory and rewards. Thus, it's a reason to count it all joy.

> Beloved, do not be surprised at the fiery trial when it comes upon you to test you, as though something strange were happening to you. But rejoice insofar as you share Christ's sufferings, that you may also rejoice and be glad when His glory is revealed. If you are insulted for

the name of Christ, you are blessed, because the Spirit of glory and of God rests upon you (1 Peter 4:12–14).

Suffering Results in God's Comfort

Paul wrote he was willing to suffer the loss of all things if that were what it took to be more like Jesus and closer to God. One thief on the cross said in essence, "Get me off this cross, and I will follow you." The other said, "If it takes this cross for me to be with you, it is worth it." If it takes suffering to be closer to God and experience more of Him and His comfort, it is well worth it. That is a great reason to count it all joy. 2 Corinthians 1:3 says, "Blessed be the God and Father of our Lord Jesus Christ, the Father of mercies and God of all comfort, who comforts us in all our affliction."

Suffering Equips to Comfort Others

Life is not to be lived on an island, but we are to be God's hands and feet spreading His kingdom to all people and nations. Therefore, the call to look for, search out, find, and comfort others with the comforts by which God has comforted us is important. Suffering lends credibility to my life so others who suffer know that God does comfort as they hear my testimony of God's comfort in suffering. This is a reason to count it all joy.

> Blessed be the God and Father of our Lord Jesus Christ, the Father of mercies and God of all comfort, who comforts us in all our affliction, so that we may be able to comfort those who are in any affliction, with the comfort with which we ourselves are comforted by God (2 Cor. 1:3–4).

Suffering Emboldens Other Christians to Advance the Gospel

Suffering is God's chosen means for the gospel to spread to all nations. As I joyfully suffer in a manner that glorifies God, other Christians see and, as a result, are infused with boldness to also proclaim the gospel. By suffering joyfully in a manner that glorifies God, there will be others who see and fearlessly respond to God's call on their lives to follow him. This is a wonderful reason to count it all joy.

> I want you to know, brothers, that what has happened to me has really served to advance the gospel, so that it has become known throughout the whole imperial guard and to all the rest that my imprisonment is for Christ. And most of the brothers, having become confident in the Lord by my imprisonment, are much more bold to speak the word without fear (Phil. 1:12–14).

Suffering Perfects God's Power

Athletes prepare to win a contest by "suffering" (training) so that, when the time comes, they can be victorious. If athletes know this maxim is true, how much more should I embrace that suffering is God's way to be more like Christ? Suffering exploits weaknesses that the power of Christ is transforming. This is indeed a reason to count suffering as joy.

> But he said to me, "My grace is sufficient for you, for my power is made perfect in weakness." Therefore I will boast all the more gladly of my weaknesses, so that the power of Christ may rest upon me (2 Cor. 12:9).

Suffering Increases Eternal Rewards

If I live to be a hundred, it is nothing compared to eternity. It is therefore better to submit to God for a short time (a lifetime) that is increasing eternal rewards than to have ease in this life. Afflictions that are "slight" (death) and "momentary" (lifetime) are but a small thing compared to what God has prepared in heaven. That indeed is a reason to count it all joy!

> So we do not lose heart. Though our outer nature is wasting away, our inner nature is being renewed day by day. For this slight momentary affliction is preparing for us an eternal weight of glory beyond all comparison, as we look not to the things that are seen but to the things that are unseen. For the things that are seen are transient, but the things that are unseen are eternal (2 Cor. 4:16–18).

Because God is accomplishing at least these things in my life, how can all things, especially suffering, not be counted joy? How much of an insult is it to push back at God when the only thing He wills and desires is His glory and my ultimate good? How much more is it right to thank God for what some consider suffering when there are at least these reasons to count everything that happens in life as joy? What we experience in life is always God calling us to walk closer with him. Embrace that those who walk the closest with God are those who suffer the most with hopeful joy for His glory!

Discussion Questions

- Paraphrase and explain James 1:2–4 in your own words.
- Which "reasons for joy" most got your attention and why?
- Were any of the author's reasons for joy hard for you to embrace? Why?
- Discuss your thoughts on the "Suffering is God's will" Bible texts.

Reflection #4: The Problem of God and Evil

My family has experienced evil perpetrated on us many times. Like others, we have been the brunt of lies and unfair treatment. (See the foreword.) I have wondered why God would allow such things into anyone's life, especially His children. I have reflected long and often for an answer from God and found it came slowly and over time as I read Scripture, listened to messages, read books, and prayed. Presented are a few thoughts for consideration about God and evil.

"The Lord has made everything for its purpose, even the wicked for the day of trouble" (Prov. 16:4). The problem of evil is not hard to understand if God is taken at His Word and we don't sit in judgment of Him. It is written in Ephesians 1:11, "In (Christ) we have obtained an inheritance… who works all things according to the counsel of His will." I'm not God so I cannot comprehend why God does whatever He chooses to do. However, from Scripture, I know God causes all things[157] to happen in the manner and way He wills them.[158] Because Proverbs 16:4 is true, God made everything, including evil people, for the day of evil as part of his master plan. Now consider the confluence of Proverbs 16:4 with Ephesians 1:11 as found in Acts 4:27–28.[159]

> For truly in this city (Jerusalem) there were gathered together against your holy servant Jesus, whom you anointed, both Herod and Pontius Pilate, along with the Gentiles and the peoples of Israel, to do whatever your hand and your plan had predestined to take place.

Regarding Jesus' death, Herod and Pilate, along with the Gentiles, Jews, and everyone else, did what God willed to happen of their own choice. God willed everything associated with Jesus' death for His glory and our good. Not one single event happened outside God's eternal plan. He willed them all for His glory to culminate in the resurrection. God did not leave salvation to chance. He made sure it would happen "so the Scripture would be fulfilled."[160] Because God doesn't change, the conclusion must be that He is working out His plan in every Christian's life, which includes hard, difficult, and sometimes evil things that He ordains as part of His plan.

Taking God at His Word from Ephesians 1:11 and Proverbs 16:4 means, in the mystery of His will, all things and people ultimately carry out His divine and perfect plan for His glory regardless of our ability to understand or comprehend His actions. Some struggle over such a thought, but it is not man's place to question God regarding what He wills and why He wills it. As Paul wrote in Romans 9:15, 19–21,

> He (God) has mercy on whomever he wills, and he hardens whomever he wills … You will say to me then, "Why does he still find fault? For who can resist His will?" But who are you, O man, to answer back to God? Will what is molded say to its molder, "Why have you made me like this?" Has the potter no right over the clay, to make out of the same lump one vessel for honored use and another for dishonorable use?

From these things, the conclusion that has comforted me is that, because God is love and only wills what is ultimately good for His children,[161] somehow beyond my understanding, even evil things that enter life can only be ultimately good when God is believed according to Romans 8:28. Therefore to question God's goodness in any event is the height of arrogance.

God's glory is the most important thing in the universe. It is God's right to determine how He is best and most glorified. If it means Him building up or tearing down, He has the right to do it. If it means granting life or taking it, He has the right to do it. If it means He sends a hurricane one place and not another, a volcano eruption at one time and not another, or a tsunami happening or not, those are His decisions. If it means one is saved and another isn't, that is His right to decide.[162] After all, everyone is commanded to repent, and if he or she doesn't, it isn't God's fault.[163]

The crucial truth is that all things and all people ultimately glorify God, even if we don't understand how it takes place. If that isn't true, then God's Word isn't true. If the Word isn't true, the Christian faith is meaningless. If the Christian faith is meaningless, Jesus is not God.

I have found believing in and trusting God, who is lovingly and absolutely providential and in sovereign control of all things, the more comfort I have knowing He will do what glorifies Himself and is ultimately good for me, no matter how I view it in the moment. I have found that taking God at His Word is vastly better and brings much more comfort than doubting Him and His goodness.

Chapter 5

WHEN GOD IS SILENT

. . . .

Right now as I write this, God seems to be silent. My heart looks to Him and strains to hear the faintest whisper from heaven, yet it seems God has chosen not to respond (yet). I don't question His love that was settled at the cross. Life is just hard right now. I need to hear from God, but I don't. He said, "Ask and it will be given to you."[164] I am, and nothing is happening. He said, "Let your requests be made known." [165] I do. And still nothing. He said, "Do not lean on your own understanding."[166] I'm trying, but it's just so hard when God seems to be silent. I feel like every prayer gets no further than the ceiling.

I've walked this path before. Many times, I have felt as though God was silent regarding my pleas. From those times of silence, I share thoughts, reflections, and ways God comforted me when He seemed to be silent.

Did that sentence hit you as odd as it did me writing it? The fact that God comforts means He is not silent. However, God could easily make an indefensible case regarding our silence toward Him in terms of anemic prayer lives than we could make regarding His supposed silence toward us. Still, our human side identifies with the psalmist who wrote, wept, and waited to hear from God.

- "I am weary with my moaning; every night I flood my bed with tears; I drench my couch with my weeping. My eye wastes away because of grief; it grows weak because of all my foes" (Ps. 6:6–7).

- "Hear my prayer, O Lord, and give ear to my cry; hold not your peace at my tears! For I am a sojourner with you, a guest, like all my fathers" (Ps. 39:12).
- "My tears have been my food day and night, while they say to me continually, 'Where is your God?' These things I remember, as I pour out my soul" (Ps. 42:3–4).
- "You have kept count of my tossings; put my tears in your bottle. Are they not in your book?" (Ps. 56:8).
- "Because of my loud groaning my bones cling to my flesh. I am like a desert owl of the wilderness, like an owl of the waste places; I lie awake; I am like a lonely sparrow on the housetop. All the day my enemies taunt me; those who deride me use my name for a curse. For I eat ashes like bread and mingle tears with my drink" (Ps. 102:5–9).

Jesus knows what it's like when God is silent. While He was on the cross, God didn't answer His own Son's pleas or cries. Because God was silent, Jesus knew his Father had forsaken him.[167] Prior to that event, the Son and Father communicated perfectly, once with others hearing God's voice themselves.[168] But in Christ's moment of most profound need, God was silent. Jesus endured God's silence so we would never have to.

God's seemingly silence tests our faith in Him because silence requires waiting. Waiting on God is not useless. However, not waiting on God is unprofitable. The children of Israel weren't willing to wait so they worshipped the golden calf, and consequently, God's judgment fell on them.[169] Because Saul didn't wait on Samuel to offer a sacrifice to God, the kingdom was taken from him.[170] By contrast, Moses was willing to wait however long it took rather than do anything without God.[171] Waiting proves faith in God and the desire for Him rather than "His stuff" (whatever we want God to do for us or give us).

What about you? How long has God seemed to be silent? Who has been silent more often, you or God? Prior to your desire or this present need to hear from God, how often have you spoken with Him in prayer just to spend time with your Father? In this situation, how long have you been asking, praying, looking to heaven, reading Scripture, and waiting to hear from God and He seems to be silent? Has it been days, weeks, months, years, or decades that God has seemed to be silent? Are you willing to pray and wait like a dear lady I know who prayed for her husband's salvation for fifty years? Whatever the length of time is, you are not the first to wait on God while He seemed to be silent. In light of 2 Corinthians 1:3–7, there are comforts God gives when he is silent. Did you get that? Written another way, God has spoken many times about when He is silent.

Consider a phrase from the hymn, "How Firm a Foundation," "What more can he say than to you he has said?" God is never silent! At any moment, we can pick up the Bible and read any of thirty-nine Old Testament books or twenty-seven New Testament books and hear God. The issue is not His silence; it's our unwillingness to hear. We think God is silent because we don't hear what He has said and has been saying. We must fine-tune our hearing sources and capabilities.

The first stanza John Rippon wrote in 1787 in "How Firm a Foundation" is "How firm a foundation, ye saints of the Lord, is laid for your faith in his excellent word! What more can he say than to you he hath said, to you who for refuge to Jesus have fled?"

These words and phrases should land in our minds like bombs: "How firm a foundation," "Ye saints of the Lord," "Is laid for your faith," and "In his excellent word!" In the Bible, God provides a firm, sure, and solid foundation for all believers. This foundation strengthens your faith, not deliver from circumstances or situations. The foundation for your faith when God seems to be silent is found in Scripture.

It could be deemed arrogant and unappreciative to accuse God of being silent. He has spoken and caused everything that will ever be needed in times of trouble and doubt to be written so the faith is strengthened. 2 Peter 1:3–4 affirms the truth Mr. Rippon wrote about in the hymn, "His divine power has granted to us all things that pertain to life and godliness, through the knowledge of Him who called us to his own glory and excellence, by which he has granted to us his precious and very great promises, so that through them you may become partakers of the divine nature."

God has already granted everything ever needed. There hasn't been, isn't, and never will be a time when God has not already provided whatever is needed in this life. If something is needed for life, it has been granted. If something is needed for the relationship to God, it has been provided. If something needs to provide comfort, it has been granted. Whatever is needed for peace, it has been granted. The problem is not the lack of provision; it's thinking God doesn't know what is needed at a given time in a particular circumstance and has not provided it. To think otherwise is astoundingly arrogant, ignorant, or both. With 2 Peter 1:3–4 in mind, what promises are believers given that pertain to "all things"? Here are a few to consider:

- "He has promised never to leave nor forsake you."[172]
- "No one can snatch you out of my Father's hand."[173]
- "God causes all things to work together for the good of those who love him, who are the called according to his purpose."[174]
- "Nothing can separate you from the love of God that is in Christ Jesus."[175]
- "God will not allow you to be tested (Tempted) above what you can handle."[176]
- "In every test, 'God will provide a way of escape to handle it.'"[177]
- "A bruised reed he will not break, and a smoldering wick he will not quench, until he brings justice to victory."[178]
- "The peace of God will guard your heart and mind."[179]
- "No good thing does he withhold from those who walk uprightly (who are in Christ)."[180]

- "He who began a good work in you will complete it."[181]
- "God who is at work in you both to will and accomplish his good pleasure."[182]

God does not promise life will be easy. He does not promise good health. God does not promise our children will become what we hope and pray for them. God does not promise our family life will be a charmed one. God does not promise our best life is now. The only thing God promises is related to our faith in Him in terms that He will "never leave or forsake us."[183] Everything else is on the table for Him to do with as he pleases for His glory and our ultimate good.

George Mueller wrote a profound statement, "Take God at His Word."[184] When you're afraid, take God at His Word. When you're confused, take God at His Word. When you feel like a failure, take God at His Word. When you have failed, take God at His Word. When others are against you, take God at His Word. When it seems He is silent, take God at His Word. In any and every circumstance, take God at His Word. There is never a situation that surprises God or is too much for him that He cannot transform into reasons to rejoice.[185] Just because it can't be seen how something can be good doesn't mean it isn't good.[186] Take God at His Word. "What more can He say than to you He has said?"

Another truth in 2 Peter 1 is almost too wonderful. Through God's promises, which means taking Him at His Word, believers partake in the divine nature. The divine nature! The divine nature! This is an amazing truth. Not that a believer is God or becomes God or a god, but somehow in the mystery of the Almighty Himself, His nature is in the believer. Meditate on what partaking of the divine nature means.

The nature of the one who created the universe lives in you. The power that overcame death after the cross is in you. The one before whom demons flee is in you. The power that holds all things together[187] is in you. The one before whom every knee will bow abides in you. The one who healed the blind, deaf, and crippled lives in you. The one who raised Lazarus from the dead lives in you. The one for whom nothing is impossible lives in you. Because God's nature is in you, your name is written down in heaven. God's Spirit bears witness with your spirit[188] that these things are true.

"What more can He say than to you He has said?" God is never silent for those who listen. He has, is, and will continue to speak to all who have ears to hear.[189] A person's inability to hear cannot be blamed on God, for He has spoken clearly to all who will listen.[190]

The axis of the universe is God's throne. Listen for what God is saying rather than what you want to hear. God knows better than you what you need, and He has provided it. The way anyone is able to hear and comprehend God is by divine revelation.[191] Hearing is not so much a matter of auditory acuity but heart sensitivity to God, His Spirit, His Son, His will, and His Word. God must make the heart able to hear what He has said. After all, for everyone who seeks and finds and everyone who knocks, the door will be opened.[192] All a person has to do to hear God is to look around and up.

> "The Heavens declare the glory of God, and the sky above proclaims his handiwork. Day to day pours out speech, and night to night reveals knowledge. There is no speech, nor are there words, whose voice is not heard" (Ps. 19:1–3).

> "What can be known about God is plain to them, because God has shown it to them. For his invisible attributes, namely, his eternal power and divine nature, have been clearly perceived, ever since the creation of the world, in the things that have been made" (Rom. 1:19–20).

In pain and hurt, people tend to look in or around rather than in at themselves and around to others instead of to God. They listen more to themselves about how difficult life is rather "than to you He has said"[193] regarding the glorious joy of how great God is in His mercy. Therein it becomes a necessity to reorient the heart by asking God to reveal Himself in what is perceived to be silence. Then, in keeping with 2 Peter 1, go to God's Word, and there the God of comfort will be found.

The actual words of Scripture are more important than anything that anyone writes about Scripture.[194] Read the texts below slowly. Meditate on each phrase. Be still while God filters his eternal truth deep into your heart. In Scripture, you will find the answer to the question posed in the hymn, "What more can He say than to you He has said?" Contemplate what He has said in His Word when it seems to you as if God is silent.

- "The eyes of all look to you, and you give them their food in due season. You open your hand; you satisfy the desire of every living thing. The Lord is righteous in all his ways and kind in all his works. The Lord is near to all who call on him, to all who call on Him in truth. He fulfills the desire of those who fear him; he also hears their cry and saves them. The Lord preserves all who love him, but all the wicked he will destroy. My mouth will speak the praise of the Lord, and let all flesh bless his holy name forever and ever" (Ps. 145:15–21).
- "I will take my stand at my watchpost and station myself on the tower, and look out to see what He will say to me, and what I will answer concerning my complaint. And the Lord answered me: 'Write the vision; make it plain on tablets, so he may run who reads it. For still the vision awaits its appointed time; it hastens to the end—it will not lie. If it seems slow, wait for it; it will surely come; it will not delay'" (Hab. 2:1–3).
- "I am the Lord; those who wait for Me shall not be put to shame" (Isa. 49:23).

- "From of old no one has heard or perceived by the ear, no eye has seen a God besides you, who acts for those who wait for him" (Isa. 64:4).
- "I will wait for the Lord, who is hiding his face from the house of Jacob, and I will hope in him" (Isa. 8:17).
- "In the path of Your judgments, O Lord, we wait for you; Your name and remembrance are the desire of our soul. My soul yearns for You in the night; my spirit within me earnestly seeks You. For when Your judgments are in the earth, the inhabitants of the world learn righteousness" (Isa. 26:8–9).
- "The Lord waits to be gracious to you, and therefore he exalts himself to show mercy to you. For the Lord is a God of justice; blessed are all those who wait for Him" (Isa. 30:18).
- "Why do you say… 'My way is hidden from the Lord, and my right is disregarded by my God'? Have you not known? Have you not heard? The Lord is the everlasting God, the Creator of the ends of the earth. He does not faint or grow weary; His understanding is unsearchable. He gives power to the faint, and to Him who has no might he increases strength. Even youths shall faint and be weary, and young men shall fall exhausted; but they who wait for the Lord shall renew their strength; they shall mount up with wings like eagles; they shall run and not be weary; they shall walk and not faint" (Isa. 40:27–31).
- "Humble yourselves, therefore, under the mighty hand of God so that at the proper time (a time of waiting) he may exalt you, casting all your anxieties on him, because he cares for you. And after you have suffered a little while (after waiting), the God of all grace, who has called you to his eternal glory in Christ, will himself restore, confirm, strengthen, and establish you. To Him be the dominion forever and ever. Amen" (1 Peter 5:6–7, 10–11).

- "And He said to all, 'If anyone would come after me, let Him deny himself and take up his cross daily and follow me. For whoever would save his life will lose it, but whoever loses his life for my sake will save it. For what does it profit a man if he gains the whole world and loses or forfeits himself?'" (Luke 9:23–26).
- "Or do you suppose it is to no purpose that the Scripture says, 'He yearns jealously over the spirit that he has made to dwell in us?' But he gives more grace. Therefore it says, 'God opposes the proud, but gives grace to the humble.' Submit yourselves therefore to God. Resist the devil, and he will flee from you. Draw near to God, and he will draw near to you. Cleanse your hands, you sinners, and purify your hearts, you double-minded" (James 4:5–8).
- "You are not your own, for you were bought with a price. So glorify God in your body" (1 Cor. 6:19–20).

Personally, after reading these passages, questions similar to those God posed to Job came to my mind about God supposedly being silent.[195] I was convicted in heart that I had ever questioned why God would not answer me quickly. Granted, it would be arrogant to equate my questions to those found in Scripture, but they helped me clear the clutter of a heart close to doubting the Almighty. God may plant other questions in your heart beyond these. If so, write them down, and consider them carefully. I asked myself the following questions and worked through them regarding God's supposed silence:

- If He wants to be silent, what is that to you? Who are you to question Him and what He wills?[196]
- If He decides to wad you up into a ball and cast you into the corner for His glory, who are you to question His decision to do so?
- If He were silent, don't you think He'd have a good reason?

you handle one-millionth of the requests He answers second? You'd melt under the pressure while He handles them all times ten million as though they are nothing.
- Because you are full of knowledge, if God did what you want, what would the outcome be, and how would you handle all the resulting consequences?
- Are you able to make yourself grow one inch, give life to the dead or sight to the blind, or make time stand still? Who then are you to doubt or question God on anything?
- You say you trust God with your eternity, yet you don't trust Him with your present. If you don't trust Him about daily things, do you really trust Him with eternity?

His Son told you something important in Matthew 6:25–34. Go read it and listen to him. Then go back to God anew.

After God placed those thoughts in my spirit, along with reading Job 38, I realized I was wrong to ever have tried to put God on the witness stand and question Him. It is one thing to want to hear from God; it is another for Him to answer like He did with Job or ignore "what to you He has said."

The only rational faith conclusion that can be embraced regarding when God is silent is that God is never silent. In fact, He has already spoken and caused to be written down everything every believer will ever need in any circumstance. Jesus suffered absolute silence from God so that those who believe in Him never experience God's silence.

God is not being silent to you in the moment or event you are in. The question is whether you are willing to hear what He is saying to you for His glory and your ultimate good. Next time you feel as though God is silent, meditate on Scripture. Drive God's truth deep into your heart so they take root. Think on them individually along with all the implications you can think of regarding your particular situation. When you struggle, reflect on these passage choosing to believe God rather than your emotions.

Discussion Questions

- What do you think is meant by God being silent?
- What are some reasons God may seem to be silent?
- Do you agree or disagree God is never silent? Why or why not?
- Explain what is meant by taking God at His Word.
- What do you think are a good help or two for when God seems to be silent?

Reflection #5: Before All Hell Breaks Loose

In my third pastorate, I encountered a severe test I was not able to overcome. I was treated unfairly and fairly at the same time. There were staunch supporters and rabid enemies. There were good, bad, and horrible days as I tried to wade through the murky waters of adversity. Truth be told, from the sixth month I was pastor, there had been one adversity after another with regular and constant tension. I had been warned not to accept the call because of how they treated ministers, but I thought I would be different. After I left, I was told the church was viewed in the state convention as "perpetually conflicted."[197] But I digress.

Year eight of my eleven-year tenure was especially difficult. Even though God had blessed more than any time in the prior 167-year history,[198] disgruntled members regularly called for me to leave. Granted, I made mistakes and gave some people sticks with which to beat me. But the constant criticism and opposition took a toll on me emotionally, spiritually, and physically. Finally, it got to the point where I either had to get hold of myself or be crushed to powder. I decided to seek God for help. (Imagine that?) The result was spending hours in personal study, not to prepare a sermon or Bible study, but to hear from God for my own spiritual and emotional health.

After a number of weeks, I settled on seven truths with personal applications. Each truth and application gave me personal comfort and peace. These were seven things I chose to believe no matter what happened or what people did or said. These were seven things I would not debate or leave open for discussion with anyone. I assigned two names for what I formulated: "Seven Hooks on Which I Hang My Hat" and "Seven Things to Nail Down before All Hell Breaks Loose." I never presented these to the church I was serving at the time, but those seven truths from God got me through many difficult days. The following are the seven hooks as I first wrote them.

They helped me to look to God to make sense of my circumstances rather than try to understand God in light of circumstances.

- **God Is Love:** Nothing bad ever has—or ever will—happen to me. Evil, yes. Bad, no (2 Cor. 1:3–6, 12:9; Rom, 8:28–a).
- **God Is Good:** It is impossible for others or me to mess up my life past God using for His glory (Ps. 73:1; Eph. 1:11).
- **God Is in Control:** God only allows into my life what is ultimately good for me (Rom. 8:28; Dan. 4:35; Isa. 46:9–10).
- **God Is Just:** Satan can only do what God allows (Ezra 9:15–A).
- **All God's Ways Are Perfect:** I rejoice in every circumstance by keeping a heaven theology (Gen. 18:25; Col 3:1–2).
- **God Is Trustworthy:** I have great hope and peace, relying upon God alone (Ps. 62:8; Isa. 42:3).
- **God Does Not Change:** My salvation and faith in God cannot be lost (Mal. 3:6; James 1:17).

Chapter 6

PRAROAFR... YOUR DESIRE IS GOD'S WILL

. . . .

When it comes to prayer, if God never answers another prayer you pray, He has answered one more than you deserve, your prayer to be saved. This thought began my most serious meditations about prayer and what my attitude should be as I pray. I am thankful God does answer prayer,[199] but the thought about not answering another prayer is worth contemplating to be thankful for every prayer He chooses to answer. Having a humble attitude toward God is always good, especially when it is related to prayer. It is with this as a foundation that praying when life is hard will be considered.

One of the requests most often presented in prayer is, "God bless us (me)."[200] Along with this request is the believer's desire to be/become more like Jesus.[201] Both are God's will for every believer. However, our definition of blessings is usually related to family, health, career, financial security, and the like. God is concerned with His glory, His children's faith, holiness, and Christ likeness. Between our desire and God's will, a significant disconnect occurs as God answers requests for blessings and conforms the believer to Christ the way He chooses, through adversity and suffering.[202]

Adversity either draws a person closer to God or drives him or her from Him. My hope is that, in adversity, you will seek God and be closer to Him through worship, Scripture, and the focus of this chapter, prayer, in particular, the kind of prayer that recognizes God for who He is and what glorifies Him while seeking those things passionately from your heart. To desire those, you will need to orient your heart for God and His glory to be supreme in all things.[203] Then will you find real joy for your soul as you pray.[204]

Let the last two paragraphs settle in your heart before reading further. Then consider God's comfort in suffering through prayer.

Years ago, I heard Dr. Chuck Swindoll say, "God doesn't use anyone He doesn't first break."[205] At the time, I strongly disagreed. Since then, Scripture, experience, and observation have confirmed Dr. Swindoll's assertion. Now my perspective is this: God's chosen method for blessing his people eternally and temporally is adversity, trial, and tribulation.[206] Because Jesus was made perfect and learned obedience through suffering,[207] the same will be true for all who follow Him.[208] Only through suffering are Christians able to share in Christ's glory, rest, and comfort.[209]

Often we ask God to remove whatever is causing our pain. We either are not aware, or have forgotten, that suffering and pain are God's ways to accomplish the request we have made to be blessed, but His blessings will always be in terms of how He defines blessing.[210] The truth is, if God had not determined for pain to accomplish His will as an ultimate good, He would not allow suffering to occur in the first place.[211] The implication should be to view difficulty as a divine providence accomplishing God's will and thus embraced as ultimately good.[212] This attitude requires submission to God[213] and taking Him at His Word over the natural inclinations of the heart.[214]

In the Model Prayer, after praising God, Jesus presents the most significant requests of the Father in prayer as, "Thy kingdom come... Thy will be done."[215] Settle those in your heart. Make them the first thoughts in your mind each morning and the last every night. Ponder long on the pervading implications of "Thy kingdom come... Thy will be done" for life in general and specific situations you experience. The deeper you drive the supremacy of God's kingdom and will into your soul, the more His peace guards your heart.[216] Trust me on this! Had I embraced these truths earlier in my life, the better able I would have been to process and handle hard times I have experienced with joy.

God's will is your joy, peace, and contentment, now and forever. The thing to remember is that He determines the best way to bring those about in your life. Even if in the moment you don't understand or see how God is working toward this goal, that does not mean it isn't true. Take Jesus at His Word as seen in the following passages:

- "Peace I leave with you; my peace I give to you. Not as the world gives do I give to you. Let not your hearts be troubled, neither let them be afraid" (John 14:27).
- "I have said these things to you, that in me you may have peace. In the world you will have tribulation. But take heart; I have overcome the world" (John 16:33).
- "Jesus said to them… 'Peace be with you. As the Father has sent me, even so I am sending you'" (John 20:21).
- "Blessed are you when people hate you and when they exclude you and revile you and spurn your name as evil, on account of the Son of Man! Rejoice in that day, and leap for joy, for behold, your reward is great in heaven" (Luke 6:22–23).
- "These things I have spoken to you, that my joy may be in you, and that your joy may be full" (John 15:11).
- "Truly, truly, I say to you, you will weep and lament, but the world will rejoice. You will be sorrowful, but your sorrow will turn into joy" (John 16:20).
- "Truly, truly, I say to you, whatever you ask of the Father in my name, he will give it to you. Until now you have asked nothing in my name. Ask, and you will receive, that your joy may be full" (John 16:23–24).
- "I am coming to you, and these things I speak in the world, that they may have my joy fulfilled in themselves" (John 17:13).

One reading of those passages is not enough. Just because you read them a time or two doesn't mean you will remember them or your heart will embrace those truths, so read them regularly. Mark them in your Bible. Memorize them.[217] For in so doing, the Spirit will bring you joy and strengthen your faith in God.[218] Take God at His Word.

T. W. Hunt wrote *Prayer Life* and *The Mind of Christ*. In 1988, he spoke at New Orleans Baptist Theological Seminary during my time there. The morning he was to speak, he brought his breakfast tray to the table where I was sitting with two friends and asked to join us. After small talk, I asked him, "Dr. Hunt, could you give us your thoughts about prayer and God's will?" He said,

> All genuine prayer begins with God who places His will as a burden on the heart of a believer to pray. Since the Christian does not know how to pray as he should, the Holy Spirit intercedes with groanings too deep for words, according to the will of God. Since the believer has no right to approach God's throne on his or her own merits, he or she prays in Jesus' name. As a result, each member of the Trinity is involved in all genuine prayer, which returns to God with whom it originated where it is always answered in the affirmative. That is my view of prayer and God's will.

We sat overwhelmed by the wisdom we had heard about prayer and God's will. This perspective has become an important truth in my understanding of prayer. Dr. Hunt helped me grasp why I pray, why I can pray, and why my prayer may or may not be answered the way I hoped or expected it to be answered.[219]

Now, as mentioned earlier, when it comes to praying during difficult times, the natural inclination of the heart is to ask for the source of pain to be removed. There is no sin in making this request, as long as the request is submitted to God's will, providence, and sovereignty. Regarding prayer and suffering, I offer four case studies for consideration. Each one provides encouragement and is worth modeling when seeking God through prayer in difficult times.

God sent Jeremiah to deliver His truth to the people of Jerusalem. While the city was under attack, Jeremiah prophesied about impending doom. The king imprisoned him for his message, even though part of the prophecy was filled with hope, joy, and blessings.[220] While in prison, with the Babylonian army about to breach the wall, Jeremiah lifted his heart toward God with these words,

> I prayed to the Lord, saying: "Ah, Lord God! It is you who has made the heavens and the earth by your great power and by your outstretched arm! Nothing is too hard for you. You show steadfast love to thousands, but you repay the guilt of fathers to their children after them, O great and mighty God, whose name is the Lord of hosts, great in counsel and mighty in deed, whose eyes are open to all the ways of the children of man, rewarding each one according to his ways and according to the fruit of his deeds. You have shown signs and wonders in the land of Egypt, and to this day in Israel and among all mankind, and have made a name for yourself, as at this day. You brought your people Israel out of the land of Egypt with signs and wonders, with a strong hand and outstretched arm, and with great terror. And you gave them this land, which you swore to their fathers to give them, a land flowing with milk and honey" ... The word of the Lord came to Jeremiah: "Behold, I am the Lord, the God of all flesh. Is anything too hard for me?" (Jer. 32:16–22, 26–27).

Jeremiah's prayer is a wonderful example of praying, "Thy kingdom come... Thy will be done." Instead of asking God to remove the threat by sending down fire from heaven or deliverance from destruction, the prophet praises and worships God. He affirms God's character and omnipotence. He recounts the great deeds of

God. Not once does he question God's wisdom, will, decisions, or providence in what is happening to him, Jerusalem, and, as a result, the nation of Israel. Jeremiah does not request deliverance or anything else for that matter. He worships, praises, glorifies, and magnifies God. That is God honoring prayer.

The lesson is regardless of the situation, circumstance, or event encountered. The main focus in prayer is God. He is to be worshipped and praised regardless of temporal circumstances. When praying in the midst of hardship, we should have Job's attitude, "Though he slay me, I will hope in him."[221] The proper attitude in prayer is to express love for God with all the heart, mind, soul, and body.[222] Then seek his kingdom and his righteousness in every life event.[223] Glorify God by trusting Him regardless of the situation or outcome,[224] supported by conduct worthy of the gospel,[225] while being salt and light to a dying world of what faith in God looks like,[226] living in peace with all people, including your enemies.[227] This is how Jeremiah prayed when it seemed to him that his life was about to end.

While these things are beyond debate as to their importance for Christian living, the ability to accomplish any of them, much less all of them together in the midst of hardship, is beyond anyone's ability. Thus, it is imperative to ask God to work in us to accomplish His will for His glory while we work with all our might to live consistent with the Word.[228] Toward this end, it is good to embrace the words of Paul from 1 Corinthians 15:10, "By the grace of God I am what I am, and his grace toward me was not in vain. On the contrary, I worked harder than any of them, though it was not I, but the grace of God that is with me."

Christians are to pray and work. Just praying isn't enough. Working hard isn't enough. It takes prayer and work while relying and trusting absolutely on God to will and accomplish His good pleasure[229] best described as holiness and conformity to Christ.[230] Keep in mind everything we do is because God gives us the ability and strength because, apart from Him, we can do nothing.[231] Then we will attain the level of maturity God wills for us.[232] If this seems too much to grasp, is beyond your ability to accomplish, or is too much to handle, I implore you to relax and de-stress by embracing Scripture.

- "Take my yoke upon you, and learn from me, for I am gentle and lowly in heart, and you will find rest for your souls. For my yoke is easy, and my burden is light" (Matt. 11:29–30).
- "By the grace of God I am what I am… I worked harder than any of them, though it was not I, but the grace of God that is with me" (1 Cor. 15:10).
- "Those whom he foreknew he also predestined to be conformed to the image of his Son" (Rom. 8:29).
- "I am sure… that he who began a good work in you will bring it to completion at the day of Jesus Christ" (Phil. 1:6).
- "God… works in you, both to will and to work for his good pleasure" (Phil. 2:13).
- "Not that we are sufficient in ourselves to claim anything as coming from us, but our sufficiency is from God" (2 Cor. 3:5).
- "[May God] equip you with everything good that you may do His will" (Heb. 13:20–21).

Now consider three examples of praying in times of stress and be encouraged. Keep the points in mind about how Jeremiah prayed as you contemplate the following.

The prophet Habakkuk lived at a time when a massive army was invading Israel. Their power and fury was overwhelming, and it was an almost certain that he would be killed in a violent manner. As he saw destruction coming, abject fear literally overcame him, causing him to have uncontrollable physical reactions. Rather than asking God to destroy the invading army or deliver him from destruction (which included total economic collapse and social breakdown), he orients his heart to worship God, much like Isaiah did when King Uzziah died.[233] Habakkuk focuses his heart on God as the ultimate unchangeable reality and rejoices in Him in the face of almost certain death. Read and embrace the power of God manifested in prayer, which is yours because the Spirit abides in you.

> I hear, and my body trembles; my lips quiver at the sound; rottenness enters into my bones; my legs tremble beneath me. Yet I will quietly wait for the day of trouble to come upon people who invade us. Though the fig tree should not blossom, nor fruit be on the vines, the produce of the olive fail and the fields yield no food, the flock be cut off from the fold and there be no herd in the stalls, yet I will rejoice in the Lord; I will take joy in the God of my salvation. God, the Lord, is my strength; he makes my feet like the deer's; he makes me tread on my high places (Hab. 3:16–19).

Like Jeremiah, Habakkuk does not ask God for deliverance, for the invaders to be destroyed, or for anything else. Instead, he is honest about his fear and orients his heart toward God in worship regardless of his circumstances or what will happen to him. Such should be the attitude of our heart when we pray. A good practice would be to actually pray this passage of Scripture back to God, asking Him to conform our heart to that Habakkuk had toward God.

Next, consider Jesus, who confessed He was experiencing emotional and spiritual turmoil that others could not fathom.[234] Christ knew that what was coming on Him was more than could be communicated by human words in that God the Father would pour out on Him eternal, pure, absolute, total, and complete wrath for the sin of every person who would ever believe.[235] Jesus knew the infinite wrath of God would be distilled and concentrated from the eternal into just three hours.[236] Along with infinite unimaginable suffering, Jesus would deal with the comparatively light physical abuses of being beaten, abandonment by all, and the scorn of those around the cross.[237] Jesus' fear shook Him to his core, causing great emotional distress manifested by sweating great drops of blood.[238] Knowing all these things, Jesus asked God to remove the cup of suffering, but only if the request were consistent with God's will. The lesson for us in prayer is to take our requests to God, always submitting to His divine will whatever it may be, including the loss of temporal life because His glory is supreme in importance.

> Taking with Him Peter and the two sons of Zebedee, He began to be sorrowful and troubled. Then He said to them, "My soul is very sorrowful, even to death; remain here, and watch with me." And going a little farther he fell on his face and prayed, saying, "My Father, if it be possible, let this cup pass from me; nevertheless, not as I will, but as you will" (Matt. 26:37–40).

It is acceptable to ask God to protect us from, remove, or end suffering, but only if it is consistent with His good, perfect, and holy will. We are to desire and pray to God, "Thy kingdom come… Thy will be done," even if it means losing everything, including our life.[239] Like Job, even though God slays you, hope is in Him[240] from a desire of the heart for His glory while submitting completely to Him so that God's will is done. This can be done because of the promise that God will eventually and ultimately bring forth glory and restoration as recorded in 1 Peter 5:6–7, 10–11.

> Humble yourselves, therefore, under the mighty hand of God so that at the proper time he may exalt you, casting all your anxieties on him, because he cares for you. (10) And after you have suffered a little while, the God of all grace, who has called you to his eternal glory in Christ, will himself restore, confirm, strengthen, and establish you. To Him be the dominion forever and ever. Amen.

Now consider Paul, who encountered more suffering than we can imagine in our safe and secure American homes. It is therefore important to give some background to understand how Paul prayed in the midst of his suffering. Once we get an idea of all that happened to Paul, then we can learn lessons about suffering and how to pray in the midst of our own hardships.

Paul was set apart from birth to live the life God ordained for him.[241] God's purpose for Paul was to suffer persecution for God's glory.[242] Paul recounts some of his difficulties in 2 Corinthians 11:23–30. Indeed, Paul did suffer many things for the gospel that most of us would never encounter. Take special note that Paul viewed suffering as affirmation he was called by God. It is proper for Christians to take the same view, that suffering is proof of God's call and not necessarily punishment from Him.

> Are they servants of Christ? I am a better one—I am talking like a madman—with far greater labors, far more imprisonments, with countless beatings, and often near death. Five times I received at the hands of the Jews the forty lashes less one. Three times I was beaten with rods. Once I was stoned. Three times I was shipwrecked; a night and a day I was adrift at sea; on frequent journeys, in danger from rivers, danger from robbers, danger from my own people, danger from Gentiles, danger in the city, danger in the wilderness, danger at sea, danger from false brothers; in toil and hardship, through many a sleepless night, in hunger and thirst, often without food, in cold and exposure. And, apart from other things, there is the daily pressure on me of my anxiety for all the churches. Who is weak, and I am not weak? Who is made to fall, and I am not indignant? If I must boast, I will boast of the things that show my weakness.

Paul knew all the things that happened to him were proof of his salvation, call, and apostleship (v. 23). Because he was imprisoned, beaten, stoned, run out of towns, and living in constant danger, he knew without a doubt that he was dead center of God's will and the Father's grace covered his life.[243] Notice some important words describing the unrelenting nature of Paul's sufferings: "Far more," "Far greater," "Five times," "Three times," "Danger" (used eight times), "Many," "Often," and "Daily."

Paul didn't just suffer an event once, but several times over the course of many years. From Paul's perspective, the phrase "slight and momentary affliction"[244] referred to death ("slight") and a lifetime ("momentary"). His daily existence wasn't a little stressful. It was dangerous. Everywhere he went, every person he encountered, and every day he lived held the possibility of suffering and death. Most everyone else would have become paranoid in a short time if he had lived Paul's life. Yet his view of what God ordained is found in 2 Corinthians 4:7–12. (Reflect on 2 Corinthians 11:23–30.)

> We have this treasure (The Gospel) in jars of clay, to show that the surpassing power belongs to God and not to us. We are afflicted in every way, but not crushed; perplexed, but not driven to despair; persecuted, but not forsaken; struck down, but not destroyed; always carrying in the body the death of Jesus, so that the life of Jesus may also be manifested in our bodies. For we who live are always being given over to death for Jesus' sake, so that the life of Jesus also may be manifested in our mortal flesh. So death is at work in us, but life in you.

Paul understood clearly that suffering was meant to exalt God, glorify Him, attribute all power to Him, and make those who suffer to rely completely on God.[245] Note to make those who suffer rely completely on Christ.[246] Among the many intents of God for our good in suffering, the best may be that it is intended for us to flee idolatry and trust God alone[247] for the purpose of Jesus being manifested in us.

Dancing in the Dungeon

Now we can consider Paul's prayer asking God to remove suffering from 2 Corinthians 12:7–10. This passage could be viewed as God's preemptive strike to prevent pride from growing in Paul.

> To keep me from being too elated by the surpassing greatness of the revelations, a thorn was given me in the flesh, a messenger of Satan to harass me, to keep me from being too elated. Three times I pleaded with the Lord about this, that it should leave me. But he said to me, "My grace is sufficient for you, for my power is made perfect in weakness." Therefore I will boast all the more gladly of my weaknesses, so that the power of Christ may rest upon me. For the sake of Christ, then, I am content with weaknesses, insults, hardships, persecutions, and calamities. For when I am weak, then I am strong (2 Cor. 12:7–10).

Paul asked God through prayer three times to remove a thorn (whatever it was). As far as we know, he didn't pray, "If it's your will, take away the thorn." It didn't matter. God always answers prayer consistent with what He determines is best anyway.[248] The thorn was God's will. Without the thorn in Paul, He would have been arrogant and full of pride (2 Cor. 12:7). Paul understood the only way he could be strong in Christ and closer to Him was for the thorn not to be removed. Given the choice of no thorn without power or a thorn with God's power and contentment, Paul chose the thorn. Paul was willing to endure a thorn, losing anything and everything in this life, in order to know Christ.[249]

What is your thorn? Would you rather the thorn be removed and lose God's power or have the thorn remain and let God continue increasing in you His power, love, grace, and mercy?

It may seem like much of what has been written thus far has little to do with how to pray when suffering, so let me make the point clear regarding prayer and suffering. God's will and desire is the same as yours, to bless you and make you more like Jesus. God does not leave either to the possibility of not happening.[250] He makes sure the events of your life conform you to the image of Christ and increase your eternal rewards.[251] The sooner you learn to trust God to accomplish these things without any possibility of failure in the manner He determines is best, the better off you will be emotionally, mentally, and spiritually. Not only that, you will also learn how to pray with God instead of in a manner that is not necessarily consistent with how prayer in adversity should take place.

There will never be a time when God is not at work both to will and accomplish His good pleasure in you. God's good pleasure is conformity to Christ. Every event in your life is designed by Him, whether you recognize it or not, to bring you into a closer relationship to Him, conform you to the image of Christ, and increase your heavenly rewards.[252]

Satan Cannot Prevent God Answering Your Prayer

In Daniel 10, the prophet had been in prayer and fasting for twenty-one days because of a vision God had given him. An angel appeared to Daniel to encourage and strengthen him and further explain the vision. The vision is not under consideration, but rather the dynamic of how the prayer was answered by God through angels. Consider what is recorded in Daniel 10:12–13, 20–21.

> Fear not, Daniel, for from the first day that you set your heart to understand and humbled yourself before your God, your words have been heard, and I have come because of your words. The prince of the kingdom of Persia withstood me twenty-one days, but Michael, one of the chief princes, came to help me… But now I will return to fight against the prince of Persia; and when I go out, behold, the prince of Greece will come. But I will tell you what is inscribed in the book of truth: there is none who contends by my side against these except Michael, your prince.

Satan and his demons are able to delay answers to prayer, but they cannot prevent God answering prayer. In this passage, the demon assigned to Persia was overcome by Michael so the answer to Daniel's prayer was delivered successfully. Then the angel had to fight the same fight again to return to heaven with Michael's help.

There are several things to embrace from this passage regarding when you pray. Sometimes when you pray, the answer is delayed because of spiritual war in heavenly places, which doesn't surprise us from Ephesians 6:12. Yet we are encouraged because "greater is he that is in you then he that is in the world,"[253] which means that neither Satan nor his demons can keep God from answering prayer. Delay the answer. Yes. Prevent the answer. No. So when an answer is delayed, keep on praying. When you wonder if God has answered you, keep on praying. Go read and learn the lesson of Luke 18:1–8 of the widow who sought justice and received it. ("Never give up" is the lesson.)

Pray in a manner consistent with what God is doing in you for your good. Pray in concert with the Holy Spirit who prays for you according to God's will.[254] When you pray, ask God to glorify Himself in you, to make you the person He desires for you to be. Ask Him to strengthen your faith and increase your knowledge of Him. Request that He give you a heart that is in tune with His heart by making you more loving, gracious, merciful, compassionate, and forgiving. Please listen closely. If you will make these things the dominating elements of your prayer life, God will grant them along with many more things you don't ask for, as Matthew 6:33 promises. Thus, it is best to pray as Jesus taught, "Thy kingdom come … Thy will be done."[255]

Discussion Questions

- What do you think of the statement, "God doesn't use anyone He doesn't first break"?

- Does it seem contradictory for peace to come through suffering? Why or why not?
- Which of the four examples of prayer in suffering was most interesting? Why?
- What is most important in prayer regarding suffering?
- What do you think of a "preemptive strike to prevent pride"?

Reflection #6: Worship as a Panacea for Discouragement

The goal of each chapter is to "comfort others with the comfort by which (I) have been comforted by God."[256] That being true, this reflection is something I rely on often in difficult times. Many Christians attest to the fact that there are few things that comforts one who is deeply discouraged like worship. By the same token, there aren't many better ways to thank God in the midst of blessings than worship. The goal of this chapter is not to give a theological treatment of worship but rather to encourage the discomforted person to worship God in all situations.

Worship is not just prayer, just reading Scripture, or just singing, but rather, it's a mixture of all three interacting with the other two. Scripture informs prayer, prayer informs singing, singing enhances Scripture, and all happens at the same time. As the three intermingle, they move fluidly one through the other without separation, distinction, or delineation. Thus, a strong prayer life and good knowledge of Scripture, along with a solid repertoire of theologically sound worship (including music), enhance each other with the culmination being worship that comforts and powerfully encourages the believer.

God vested music with great power. It can excite, strengthen, and lift hearts to the portals of heaven in difficult times. When King Saul was depressed, David would play music, and the king was comforted.[257] King David wept, prayed, and fasted for the healing of the child Bathsheba bore to him. But when the child died, David went to the House of God and worshipped.[258] After the Last Supper and before going to pray in the garden of Gethsemane, Jesus sang a hymn with the eleven apostles.[259] When Paul and Silas were beaten, thrown into a dungeon, and chained, they were praying and singing at about midnight. They were "dancing in the dungeon."[260] Last, let it not be missed that psalms are songs of worship that believers have turned to over the centuries for encouragement.

As to the particulars and specifics of private worship, there are three elements for consideration. First, there is no substitution for regular, systematic, and comprehensive reading of God's Word. Read Scripture from Genesis to Revelation often. The best way to read Scripture is not for speed in order to complete a certain number of chapters a day, but rather read to encounter God by his revelation for understanding and knowing him. Thus, the suggestion is to read slowly. Along with reading slowly, read the same portion of Scripture several times. Along with reading Scripture slowly and the same passage several times, meditate on specific passages that God's Spirit impresses on your heart and drive them deep into your soul. As it is written, "Thy Word have I hid in my heart that I may not sin against you."[261]

Second, as with reading Scripture, there is no substitution for a regular and strong prayer life. Someone wrote the truest test of who we are is what we do when no one is watching. This thought comes from Jesus who taught that prayer was a matter best done in private.[262] The more often a person prays, the stronger his or her prayer life will become and be. From the gospels, it is known Jesus prayed often.[263] It is recorded that Anna stayed in the temple all day every day in fasting and prayer.[264] Hannah, the prophet Samuel's mother, was powerful in prayer.[265] Daniel prayed three times a day.[266] James wrote, "The effectual fervent prayer of a righteous man is powerful."[267] Then it is written to pray without ceasing.[268]

The third element of worship is singing and music. Over the years, God has brought a number of songs that spoke to me in different ways into my life. Along the way, I have added a song here and another there, including renditions from different artists. Genre means little to me. I am concerned most with the theology and impact they have in my heart at a given time. The following is a short list of songs God has used to encourage, comfort, strengthen, and embolden me. I encourage you find these and listen to them. Or more importantly, pull together songs that engage your heart in worship through prayer, Scripture, and music.

Note: The first song is the one God has used most powerfully in my life.

- "I Asked the Lord That I Might Grow" (John Newton, T4G, Bob Kaughlin)[269]
- "Already There" (Casting Crowns)
- "The Well" (Casting Crowns)
- "Voice of Truth" (Casting Crowns)
- "I Will Trust in You" (Jeremy Camp)
- "All My Fountains" (Travis Cottrell)
- "We Will Dance" (Travis Cottrell)
- "All I Have Is Christ" (Bob Kaughlin)
- "When I Survey the Wondrous Cross" (Bob Kaughlin, T4G)
- "All Hail the Power Of Jesus' Name" (4 Him)
- "There Is a Fountain" (4 Him)
- "It Is Well with My Soul" (4 Him)
- "Give Me Jesus" (Fernando Ortega)
- "How Firm a Foundation" (Fernando Ortega)
- "My Finest Hour" (Matthew West)
- "I Then Shall Live" (Gaither Vocal Band)
- "He'll Welcome Me" (Brooklyn Tabernacle Choir)
- "One Less Stone" (Brooklyn Tabernacle Choir)
- "Heaven Medley" (Brooklyn Tabernacle Choir)
- "All About You" (Lakewood)
- "Better Than Life" (Lakewood)

These are my top twenty-one. There have been many times while driving and listening to these songs that I have wept with joy and had hopeful expectation of Christ's return with my heart lifted from deep sorrow. My best encouragement is for you to consider the suggestions presented here and go to God through prayer, Scripture, and singing (worship) to find the peace and comfort only He provides.

Another element of worship that has comforted me is exercise.[270] Taking care of the temple that God has given us is important.[271] To ignore the body by focusing just on the soul or mind is like trying to sit on a two-legged stool. Regular exercise means thirty minutes a day at least four or five days a week. When we exercise, God made our body so as to release endorphins that aid in emotional health. Also don't forget to eat well, like vegetables, fruit, fiber, and so forth. Diet and exercise are of tremendous importance to be able to dance in the dungeon.

CHAPTER 7

ATTITUDE AND REST FOR THE SOUL

A friend used to say often, "Attitude is everything." While I agreed with him, I found it near impossible to will a good attitude just because "attitude is everything." I found it difficult to have a good attitude when life pressed in on me. For me, having a good attitude because "attitude is everything" was like trying to will away a toothache. I couldn't do it. It was impossible, so I felt defeated.

After trying to will in myself a good attitude for a while, I got tired of failing. I concluded that, to have a good attitude, I needed help, divine help specifically. I didn't just want to have a good attitude. I wanted to be the kind of person who had a good attitude because it was natural and not something I projected to others by force of my will.

As I reflected on the difference between willing a good attitude and naturally having a good attitude, I thought of Jesus' interaction with the woman at the well recorded in John 4. Jesus asked her for water to drink. Then ensued a conversation about the oddity of a Jew (Jesus) asking a Samaritan woman for water. Jesus told her, if she knew who He was, she would have asked Him for living water so as to never thirst again. Jesus described the living water he offered in John 4:13–14, "Jesus said to her, 'Everyone who drinks of this water will be thirsty again, but whoever drinks of the water that I will give

Him will never be thirsty forever. The water that I will give Him will become in Him a spring of water welling up to eternal life.'"

The two words "in Him" described what I needed and wanted in order to have a good attitude. I wanted a good attitude to be who I was rather than something I willed or projected to others. I wanted a good attitude to be real and lasting, unaffected by events or circumstances. At the same time, I innately knew there was no way I could bring it about. It would take someone more capable than I was to make it happen, and the only person with that power was God.

A good attitude can be willed temporarily, but sooner or later, the human will fails. Conversely, what Jesus gives is supernatural, eternal, and powerful. His power is implanted in a person by the Holy Spirit. As a result, the person naturally has in him or her life, eternal life, a God-driven good attitude. What Jesus gives is not affected by external forces because it is from God, divinely planted inside the individual. What Jesus gives can never be lost, taken, or removed. Having this kind of "good attitude" is evidence of a soul at rest in God.

It is no secret that life is tough for everyone. All people, families, companies, institutions, governments, and cultures are broken by sin. There is heartache everywhere, which makes it difficult to have a good attitude. However, Jesus makes either an outlandish and unbelievable claim or the most wonderful promise anyone has ever made. He promises absolute, total, and complete rest for every soul who comes to Him. In human terms, He promises a good attitude that springs up from within.

As I meditated on these things, it occurred to me that God desires for me what I longed for. Call it a good attitude, living water, or whatever you wish. God works those things in His children. It is called conformity to Christ in Romans 8:29. Paul describes the process in Philippians 2:13, "For it is God who works in you, both to will and to work for his good pleasure." God's good pleasure is for the believer to become more like His Son over the course of his or her life, which results in rest for the soul.

God has inexhaustible power to bring about peace, joy, and contentment for all who desire it, and it is free to all. They all can be purchased without money.[272] Only faith and belief are required for God to open the windows of heaven and pour out his blessings that cannot be contained. Toward this end, Jesus issues a universal call for everyone to receive from Him spiritual rest in Matthew 11:28–30. "Come to me, all who labor and are heavy laden, and I will give you rest. Take my yoke upon you, and learn from me, for I am gentle and lowly in heart, and you will find rest for your souls. For my yoke is easy, and my burden is light."

Like the woman at the well, Jesus calls every person to come to Him to find eternal rest for his or her soul, which will result in being the kind of person who has a good attitude. Age or ethnic background doesn't matter. Education is not required. Political affiliation makes no difference. There are no background checks or credit reports. It doesn't matter if a person is law abiding or on death row. It matters not whether a person is of high social standing or an outcast. Jesus offers every person who labors or is heavy laden by the difficulties of this life to find rest for his or her soul.

Those who labor unceasingly for recognition but are unknown are offered rest. Those who labor to get ahead but keep losing ground are offered rest. Those who labor for love but find themselves alone are offered rest. Those who labor to be accepted but are ignored are offered rest. Those who labor for peace but can't find it are offered rest. Jesus calls all to come and find rest for their soul in Him.

Who all is called?

- Those who carry burdens of anxiety, fear, worry, uncertainty, and loneliness
- Those who carry burdens that weigh down the soul at night in bed, when driving, or when alone
- Those who feel hopeless, helpless, and depressed

- Those with mountainous problems so far above them that they feel like they're at the bottom of the ocean trying to jump over Mount Everest with one leap

These are the people Jesus calls to come to Him, and He will give them the rest so desperately desired and needed.

Can it happen? Can Jesus give peace to anyone, regardless of his or her circumstances? Is it possible for absolutely anyone without exception to have rest to the depths of his or her soul? The answer is yes to all those questions. Consider the following:

- "Is anything too hard for the Lord?" (Gen. 18:14).
- "The Lord's hand is not shortened, that it cannot save, or his ear dull, that it cannot hear" (Isa. 59:1).
- "Truly, I say to you, if you have faith like a grain of mustard seed, you will say to this mountain, 'Move from here to there,' and it will move, and nothing will be impossible for you" (Matt. 17:20).
- "Jesus looked at them and said, 'With man this is impossible, but with God all things are possible'" (Matt. 19:26).
- "Nothing will be impossible with God" (Luke 1:37).
- "What is impossible with men is possible with God" (Luke 18:27).
- "Now to Him who is able to do far more abundantly than all that we ask or think, according to the power at work within us" (Eph. 3:20).

No matter how heavy a burden is, God can lift it and grant His peace. No matter how long a person has labored unsuccessfully to find rest for his or her soul, God can and will give peace that surpasses all understanding and comprehension.[273] Regardless of how impossible it may seem for a life to be turned from hopelessness to being filled with absolute, all-pervading joy, God through Jesus Christ can and will accomplish it for those who come to Him.

According to Jesus in Matthew 11:28–30, He is the source of rest for the soul. His rest is deep, abiding, and constant and cannot ever be lost regardless of the situation or circumstance. Natural disasters cannot affect it. Societal unrest cannot steal it. Personal problems are never so powerful as to minimize it. In Jesus, the deepest longings of the soul are fulfilled to overflowing. In Jesus, every worry is eradicated. In Jesus, there will never be anything that through Him the Christian cannot overcome with abundant, perfect, and lasting joy, peace, and rest.

1 Peter 5:6–7 supports Matthew 11:28–30 perfectly. Peter wrote, "Humble yourselves, therefore, under the mighty hand of God so that at the proper time he may exalt you, casting all your anxieties on him, because he cares for you."

Peter, the apostle who failed Christ by denying Him three times, encourages casting all your anxieties on Jesus. Why? Because He cares for you. Jesus cares for those who have failed, sinned, or blown it multiple times, along with those who are weak and made mistakes and bad decisions. Jesus cares for those who are emotionally, physically, and spiritually burdened and heavy laden. Jesus cares for every hurting and wounded soul and will give complete rest to all who come to Him. Peter knows because he had firsthand experience when Jesus restored him after his personal failure.[274]

I have found rest for my soul by reflecting deeply and often on God's truth, regardless of my circumstances. I have found rest for my soul when I took and kept on taking my problems, pain, fear, and troubles to God through prayer. I have found rest by going to God through personal worship. When it comes to prayer there is only one way to benefit from it and that is by praying. If you don't pray you certainly won't get anything out of that. I have come to the conclusion that, in my clouded view of life, I cannot know or discern how much God has been supporting and encouraging me through the spiritual disciplines, but I knew there was no hope for me if I turned away from God by not worshipping, praying, and reflecting on Scripture. So I have chosen to keep on going to Jesus, taking Him at His Word from Matthew 11:28–30.

The way to respond to Jesus' call from Matthew 11:28–30 is constant, daily surrender to Him through the spiritual disciplines (prayer, Scripture reading, and worship). Much like the person with high blood pressure has to exercise daily, watch his or her diet daily, and take his or her medicine daily, so it is more important for the believer to keep on worshipping, praying, reflecting on Scripture, and staying surrendered to Christ. He promises that, when we go to Him, we will find rest for our soul. Take Jesus at His Word.

Discussion Questions

- How does John 4:13–14 relate to having a good attitude and rest for the soul?
- How would you describe "rest for the soul"?
- What is meant by "rest for the soul"?
- How do Genesis 18:14 and 1 Peter 5:6–7 relate to one another?

Reflection #7: Waiting on God… Keeping a Biblical Perspective

One struggle every Christian can identify with is waiting on God. In a society that places high value on action, inactivity (waiting) is frustrating and viewed by some as a character flaw. This is compounded when, while waiting, something deemed to be bad or evil transpires. The natural tendency is to think the negative event wouldn't have happened if the person had acted in a timely fashion rather than waste time waiting. Such is not the case with God.

Waiting does not mean inactivity. A waiter or waitress doesn't just sit. He or she is busy serving his or her customers. Likewise, the Christian who waits on God is not to just sit as he or she waits. There are many good things he or she can and should do. Waiting does not preclude praying, worshipping, serving others, or doing a host of things. While waiting on God, it is good to be active in doing as much as possible to prepare yourself for when God does move and act in your life. As athletes are sometimes put on a bench to rest so as to go back into the game, likewise, believers are sometimes put on the sideline of life to rest and be rejuvenated so that, when the time comes, they are ready to reenter the game. Rest and wait while benched, be busy working, prepare, and strengthen yourself because, in God's time, you'll reenter the game.

There are some attributes waiting with being lazy or inept, but this is not necessarily so. It may look like a mother hen sitting on a nest of eggs is being inactive, but she is providing a necessary function to sustain life to her chicks still in the egg. How much more so is this true for the one who waits on the all wise and sovereign God, the one who "works all things after the counsel of His will,"[275] who does not withhold anything He deems good from His children?[276]

God's wise, redeeming love is completely compatible with waiting, and while waiting, evil things are happening in your life. God's loving wisdom can take decades before He reveals His good intents and purposes. God doesn't work in terms of hours, weeks, or months as much as He works in terms of years, decades, centuries, and eternity.

Consider Joseph's life timeline as found in Genesis. He had to wait on God for years to fulfill a dream given to him when he was young, and while waiting for it to be fulfilled, a number of seemingly bad things happened to him. Yet those who reflect deeply on Joseph's life will know that, unless each event happened as it did and when it did, the end result would not have resulted in many good things for two nations and Joseph's family.

Joseph was seventeen years old when his story begins in Genesis 32:7. His dysfunction and that of his family resulted in God acting to redeem his family and him, keep many people alive, and perpetuate the Messianic line so Christ would be born and all who believe would be saved.[277] Joseph was attacked by his brothers who hated him and wanted to kill him. They sold him into slavery to Midianites, who sold him to Potipher in Egypt, whose wife falsely accused him of rape. He was then thrown into prison and forgotten for two years by men who promised not to forget him so as to aid Joseph's release. These events transpired over the course of thirteen years.

Finally, when Joseph was thirty years old, he was elevated to second in power under Pharaoh in Egypt.[278] Then this began seven years of plenty as grain was stored up in preparation for seven years of famine.[279] At some point during the seven years of famine, Joseph's brothers came asking for grain. By that time, Joseph was in his forties, possibly around forty-four years old, when life started making sense to him. Now think about a few things.

It is difficult to find any direct mention of God in the narrative about Joseph and the events from Genesis 32:7 until Genesis 50:20. It isn't recorded that God revealed to Joseph His purposes in all the evil that happened to him. For thirteen years, Joseph endured evil with the very real possibility of God's silence from heaven. Joseph was seventeen when his troubles began, and there was not a resolution and restoration with his family until he was about forty-four years old. God's work of redemption and blessing took twenty-seven years. For almost three decades, Joseph was mistreated and suffered horribly. Yet he was faithful and trusted God through it all.

Consider if every event in Joseph's life had not happened the way it did at the time it did. The Messianic line would have ended, and salvation would not have been possible. Likewise, God is just as much at work in your life as a believer, and you may not be aware of it in the moment. However, you have the story of Joseph to understand what he did not know, namely, God is at work in your life for His glory and your good.[280]

You may be in year one, ten, or thirteen of God working His plan for your life. Keep on keeping on. Stay faithful to God. Honor Him, and He will honor you.[281] Take God at His Word. You won't know until and if God chooses to reveal what He has been doing in and around you. That is why we live each day by faith.[282] No matter what is happening to, in, and around you, no matter how difficult it may be, even if God does not seem to be doing anything, remember that "a bruised reed He will not break, and a smoldering wick He will not quench, until He brings justice to victory."[283]

Chapter 8

COMFORT WHEN BETRAYED

. . . .

The most infamous betrayal in history is Judas with Jesus. No other person committed a more scandalous act of disloyalty than when Judas' kiss gave Christ, the Son of God, over to the Romans.[284] Thus, the least of the apostles will forever have committed the most atrocious act of betrayal in human history. Nothing done by any human will ever come close. That being said, it is worth noting that, when betrayal takes place in our lives, Christ modeled the response we are to follow. He didn't strike out at Judas, but He submitted to the event as God's providence to bring about salvation.[285] As has been said, "Jesus didn't suffer so that we wouldn't suffer, but so that when we suffer we would be like him."

What I write in this chapter about betrayal comes from my experiences.[286] I have not been betrayed in exactly the same way you have or possibly will be. Consequently, I trust what I write about betrayal will be applied by the Holy Spirit to the circumstances you encounter.

Adultery is likely the deepest act of betrayal anyone can experience. Next may be when one family member turns on another one (parent against child, child against parent, sibling against sibling, and so forth). Next would most likely be when friends turn on each other. Regardless of the context, betrayal is betrayal, which wounds individuals to varying degrees.

It is no surprise to us when an unbelieving stranger is the betrayer, but when it is a brother or sister in Christ, the hurt is unexpected, surprising, and devastating. Christians know being betrayed is how things happen in a world full of unbelievers, but getting stabbed in the back by family or a fellow Christian upsets the apple cart more than usual. Paul wrote about betrayal.

> Alexander the coppersmith did me great harm; the Lord will repay Him according to his deeds. Beware of Him yourself, for he strongly opposed our message. At my first defense no one came to stand by me, but all deserted me. May it not be charged against them! But the Lord stood by me and strengthened me, so that through me the message might be fully proclaimed and all the Gentiles might hear it. So I was rescued from the lion's mouth. The Lord will rescue me from every evil deed and bring me safely into his heavenly kingdom. To Him be the glory forever and ever. Amen (2 Tim. 4:14–18).

This is a wonderful passage from which God provides several comforts regarding betrayal. Without going into great detail, note a few things worth reflection. Take these thoughts, and work them into your heart when you are betrayed. Ask God to help you embrace Him and fill you with the Spirit so as to rest in Him based on His truth. These thoughts have helped me with my perspective and attitude when I have been betrayed:

- Paul left vengeance and revenge in God's hands.
- Paul warned others about those who cause trouble.
- Even when deserted by everyone, Paul didn't hold a grudge.
- Paul's strength came from Christ, not people.
- Paul recognized having to rely on Christ alone was best for the gospel.

Paul was confident of God rescuing him defined as entering heaven. In other words, ultimate deliverance is when we are with Christ in heaven. Until then, there are no absolute promises. As a result, Paul praised God for how this situation (betrayal) was played out by God.

Most of the wounds I have experienced took place in the context of Christ followers in a local church. This has helped to keep Ephesians 6: 12 in mind, "We do not wrestle against flesh and blood, but against the rulers, against the authorities, against the cosmic powers over this present darkness, against the spiritual forces of evil in the heavenly places." While this passage is certainly true, it does not diminish the pain of a brother or sister in Christ saying and/or doing things that hurt deeply.

False accusations from others have wounded my family and me deeply. Several times, I vacillated between calling people down in public, implementing church discipline,[287] confronting them with others as witnesses, and, I embarrassingly have to admit, desiring that something bad happen to them so they would learn a lesson.[288]

But then, a number of Bible truths settled into my mind and worked their way deeper into my heart than I anticipated. The Spirit brought God's Word alive in my soul and seemed to ask, "Will you follow me now when it is hard, or will you just preach these things?" I realized I couldn't preach what I didn't live. I reflected on the following passages while dealing with the hurt of betrayal:

- "Do not resist the one who is evil. But if anyone slaps you on the right cheek, turn to Him the other also" (Matt. 5:39).
- "Love your enemies and pray for those who persecute you, so that you may be sons of your Father who is in heaven" (Matt. 5:44–45).
- "Repay no one evil for evil, but give thought to do what is honorable in the sight of all. If possible, so much as it depends on you, live peaceably with all. Beloved, never

avenge yourselves, but leave it to the wrath of God" (Rom. 12:17–19).
- "Let all bitterness and wrath and anger and clamor and slander be put away from you, along with all malice. Be kind to one another, tenderhearted, forgiving one another, as God in Christ forgave you" (Eph. 4:31–32).
- "Whatever happens, conduct yourselves in a manner worthy of the gospel of Christ" (Phil. 1:27) (NIV).

The phrase, "as much as it depends on you" from Romans 12, was often on my mind. It didn't matter what others said or did. What mattered was how I conducted myself. Regardless of what other people did or didn't do, regardless of how situations present themselves, no matter the injustice of circumstances, those do not change how I am to conduct myself.[289] There are no exceptions, no caveats, and no extenuating circumstances. I was either to be obedient to the gospel or tattoo myself as a hypocrite. While it was hard at first to embrace the scriptural requirements, the more I reflected, the easier it was to want to keep them. The way God works to conform us to the image of Christ and live for Him was spoken in the High Priestly prayer by Jesus, "Sanctify them in the truth; Your Word is truth."[290]

At one point when I was lamenting the hurt of accusations when my wife (now affectionately called Nathan from 2 Samuel 12) said something I will never forget, "If we believe what we say we believe, how can we be angry with the people God is using to conform us into the image of Christ?" I felt like David must have when Nathan pointed at him and said, "You are the man!"[291] She was right. I had lost my perspective regarding Romans 8:28–29 that God causes all things, including slander, lies, and betrayal, to work together for His glory and our good. I had forgotten that God is so determined to conform us to the image of Christ (our ultimate good) that He does not leave our sanctification to chance.[292] He wills it, and that includes being betrayed by others.

At some point later, I received an email that I changed, edited, and rewrote to reflect my theology and perspective directly related to what my wife said. I retitled it, "Enemies as Emissaries of God's Grace." Since then, I have often returned to it for a reminder of God's work, not only in me, but everyone who is betrayed.

So what is the conclusion? I meditate on several things when anyone, believer or unbeliever, betrays me. By following them, I have found peace now that promises peace when I stand before God on judgment day.[293] Consider these things when you are betrayed while remembering Jesus' command, "If anyone would come after me, he must deny himself and take up his cross daily and follow me."[294]

- In all things, God is working to make you more like Jesus.[295]
- The Spirit will empower you to be obedient to Scripture.[296]
- Obedience means turning the other cheek to your enemy.
- Obedience means loving and praying for your enemy.
- Obedience is being peaceful with others at all times.
- Obedience is never taking revenge but leaving it to God.
- Obedience is being kind to and forgiving your enemy.
- Obedience is always conducting yourself in a manner worthy of the gospel.
- The result will be hearing God say, "Well done, good and faithful servant!"[297]

There is one person each person is responsible for, himself or herself. No one can control anyone else regarding what he or she does or says. However, the Christian is, by the Holy Spirit's power, able to live in a manner worthy of the gospel. Christians are to live this life just to live again in heaven with the goal of hearing God say to them, "Well done. Well done, good and faithful servant!"

In closing, meditate long on 1 Corinthians 4:2–5.

> Moreover, it is required of stewards that they be found trustworthy. But with me it is a very small thing that I

should be judged by you or by any human court. In fact, I do not even judge myself. I am not aware of anything against myself, but I am not thereby acquitted. It is the Lord who judges me. Therefore do not pronounce judgment before the time, before the Lord comes, who will bring to light the things now hidden in darkness and will disclose the purposes of the heart. Then each one will receive his commendation from God.

Discussion Questions

- Discuss a definition of what betrayal is and why and how it happens.
- Have you ever betrayed anyone? Were you justified in doing so?
- Discuss Paul's thoughts regarding Alexander's betrayal.
- Which of the five passages the author presented about handling betrayal most affected you? Why?
- What do you think of the author's wife's statement?

Reflection #8: Enemies as Emissaries of God's Grace

If I keep a heavenly perspective and believe Romans 8:28 that enemies are not really enemies, they are the best friends I have. What is meant by some to hurt actually brings about a work of grace in me that wouldn't take place any other way. It has been said that, if it takes an enemy to tell you the truth, you have no friends.[298] That is a true statement.

There can be no perfection in God's children without the chastising work of God the Father.[299] When a supposed enemy attacks, God exposes sinful blind spots hidden in my heart. When friends extol my virtues and praise me from a heart of friendship, I appreciate their expressions of love, but it is more important to be told truth even when it wounds me deeply. Otherwise, I will not be working to become more like Christ, and the blind spots I have will grow and infect my soul.[300]

When a person I perceive as an enemy shames me in some way, there rises up a defensive spirit of "righteous indignation" to refute the enemy (to my detriment). Then the Spirit does His work and exposes my sin to me in an undeniable way. Then I see things I either did not know were present or I had ignored. Then I see my faults, failures, and shortcomings. I see my blind spots.

If I repent, God delivers me from what has been exposed in my heart, what was hidden and lying dormant until He used a supposed enemy to expose it. Then the process of crucifying my prideful sin begins, a course that God continues in me as long as I live. This process never takes place unless the pain of seeing my sin is facilitated by some kind of wound. But what is intended by supposed enemies for evil, God intends for good.[301]

There is residual sin in my life, sin I enjoy and protect that are better known as idols. These are things I would never address without being forced to address in some way. There are lessons I must learn that can only be learned by the crucible of adversity, pain, and difficulty. God uses those I perceive as enemies to expose things in my life that otherwise would never be seen, much less removed from my life. What some call an enemy is really a best friend, a helper, an emissary from God for my good. For the way to Christ likeness is the cross, and the navigator God uses to direct me are those some call enemies.

Jesus couldn't nail himself to the cross. His friends would never have done it. His apostles would have refused to do it. So it ended up his enemies, under the direction of Christ's archenemy Satan, who was under the complete control of God, did what no one else would do.[302]

Had the archenemy known that what he was doing would bring about Jesus' glory and salvation for all who'd believe, he never would have nailed Jesus to the cross. He didn't know what he intended for destruction was the means God ordained for glorification.

I am reluctant to crucify myself. Friends will not do it. It takes a person who is perceived as an enemy to nail me to a metaphorical cross. This person has to do something and, as a result, be perceived as an enemy by nailing me to a cross. In God's wisdom, He has determined that a cross is the only way His children will become more like His Son and the holiness that is required to see Him.[303] Without people doing what they think will hurt or destroy me, I would never become more like Jesus. They are a required part of sanctification. Thus, I must see them as some of my best friends.

Not to draw too close a comparison between Jesus' cross and my piddling problems, but if my supposed enemies knew the renewal and strengthening their actions would have, they probably wouldn't want to help me so much. The prayer I have is not to work against my supposed enemies, but with God.

This perspective is a great help in being able to apply Jesus' words to "love your enemies." For in reality, they are not enemies, but emissaries of transformation, reformation, restoration, holiness, godliness, and hope. As I look to see God's hand in the moment (rather than in hindsight), I realize my supposed enemies are unwitting professors in the school of holiness. They teach humility, brokenness, and mercy. They instruct me in righteousness, holiness, and grace. Without these supposed enemies, I would not grow in faith and share in God's holiness.[304] Without them, I would continue in darkness and never move toward God desiring to be more like Jesus.

So in reality, I have no enemies, except one who is called Satan. The worst attacks leveled against me, the deepest wounds to my heart, and the most devastating criticisms thrown my way all fall under the providential hand of God.[305] When I submit to the Father of Spirits, I live.[306] For this reason, I work toward appreciating, loving, and being thankful for those who supposedly attempt to hurt or destroy me.

It can be said with confidence, given this perspective on life, it is impossible for other people to mess up my life because God is doing a greater work. God only allows Satan to do what accomplishes the opposite of what Satan intends. God uses Satan to conform me to the image of Christ, which is the opposite of what he seeks in attacking me.

Without discipline manifested through the work of my supposed enemies, I would not work fervently and diligently to become more like Christ. Unless there were people who filled the role of a supposed enemy, I wouldn't see my sin or do anything to address it for the purpose of crucifying it.

When I submit to the loving hand of discipline from the Father, I'll become more like Jesus. I'll be one more step closer to glory. I'll be able to move on to the next level in my walk with God. I'll be better prepared to face the next work that God wills to conform me to the image of His Son. I'll be better prepared to deal with the next situation that will come, once again, from a supposed enemy. When I work with God instead of against Him, the result will be righteousness and peace in His presence.[307]

In reality, the truth is, through persecution, a supposed enemy only sets fire to the hay, wood, and stubble that would be burned up.[308] What they intend for evil is purifying the silver, gold, and precious stones of my heart. This is why I say that others cannot mess up my life because what they perceive as hurting me is actually helping me become more like Jesus.[309]

So I thank God for supposed enemies and pray that I will continue to do so. I pray I will fan the flame of what can be burned so that what cannot burn will stand forever to the glory of God.

CHAPTER 9

COMFORT IN PERSONAL FAILURE

. . . .

This is a hard chapter to write as I once again replay memories of personal failures. But I'm confident God will be faithful to comfort me anew. More importantly, I am hopefully convinced the Lord will work in you to view your personal failures as He does. My prayer is that you will encounter God as you work through the guilt of personal failure. Portions of this chapter may be hard to read, but remember, "For the moment all discipline seems painful rather than pleasant, but later it yields the peaceful fruit of righteousness to those who have been trained by it."[310]

It is one thing to deal with hardship and difficulty from others or a result of living in a broken world. It is another to suffer because of your own mistakes, failures, and sin. I regret the mistakes I've made from ignorance, foolishness, and callousness. I have said and done things that gave people sticks with which to beat me. At times, my attitude has been improper, and I have suffered as a result with no one to blame but myself. I have replayed mistakes I've made in my mind, beat myself up for being so rebellious toward God, and hurt those around me, especially those I love. You may have experienced some of these things yourself. If so, know there is hope and God will comfort you.

Eventually, you will fail because of a decision, series of decisions, lack of a decision, something you did or didn't say, or anything you did or didn't do. In those times, remember that God's grace, forgiveness, and comfort always exceed your failures.[311] When you fail, repent and be reconciled with God and whoever you have offended.[312] To do anything else is dangerous for you, your family, and others.

Not to forgive yourself by embracing God's forgiveness for your personal failure is emotionally and spiritually catastrophic, lighting the fires of hell within the soul that singe those around you. I have looked at the face and into the eyes of one who carried the guilt of personal failures from decades of bad decisions and conduct. It was a horrible sight to behold. Admitting personal failure and sin is one of the most difficult things anyone will ever do.

A man I knew professed to be a Christian and had served three churches as their pastor. Eventually, he left the ministry and lived for years in rebellion to God.[313] He thought he could sin and avoid the consequences.[314] In his youth, he was charismatic, gregarious, popular, and full of life. But by the time he reached his seventies, he sat at his kitchen table daily, staring into space for hours, blaming everyone else because (in his mind) they were the cause of his condition. He was angry and resentful, bitterly loathing himself and almost everyone else. His final years were spent in a drunken stupor, longing to die so his life would just be over. He knew God forgave intellectually, but to my knowledge, he never asked anyone to forgive him for anything, and he didn't forgive anyone, including himself. This man was my dad.

If he had believed what he read in Scripture and taught others, taken God at His Word regarding repentance and forgiveness, agreed with God that he had sinned and asked God to forgive him, repented and asked others to forgive him, and moved the Scripture eighteen inches from his head to his heart, how different his life would have been. He could have lived in peaceful joy in spite of his personal failures.[315] Of course, the best path he should have followed is the same we should strive for, which is to avoid sin and flee it.[316]

When you fail, embrace God's love through Jesus and the forgiveness He provides.[317] Read 1 John 3:19-21, and memorize and quote it often because you never know when the memory of a past failure will pop into your mind to steal your joy. Meditate long on these words of comfort and peace.

> By this we shall know that we are of the truth and reassure our heart before (God); for whenever our heart condemns us, God is greater than our heart, and he knows everything. Beloved, if our heart does not condemn us, we have confidence before God (1 John 3:19–21).

There is another thought to present you before examining personal failure. Rejoice and thank God for the times you did not fail. Consider God has prevented you from failing and you didn't know it. There have been times when he intervened in your life, heart, and mind and kept you from failing and you were unaware of his protection.[318] Such is not only a possibility, but a certainty and supported by Scripture.

In Genesis 20, Abraham and Sarah came to a land ruled by Abimelech, who desired Sarah to be in his harem. In fear of the king, Abraham and Sarah lied, saying she was his sister. Based on this statement, Abimelech took Sarah into his harem. It is recorded in Genesis 20:3–6 that God spoke to Abimelech in a dream about Sarah, how close he was to death, and what God did to prevent sin.

> God came to Abimelech in a dream by night and said to him, "Behold, you are a dead man because of the woman whom you have taken, for she is a man's wife." Now Abimelech had not approached her. So he said, "Lord, will you kill an innocent people? Did he not himself say to me, 'She is my sister?' And she herself said, 'He is my brother.' In the integrity of my heart and the innocence of my hands I have done this." Then God said to Him in the dream, "Yes, I know that you have done this in the integrity of your heart, and it was I who kept you

from sinning against me. Therefore I did not let you touch her."

Without going into detail, one point of the text is that God kept the king from doing what he would have done, sinfully sleeping with Sarah, without ever violating the king's will. Had God not revealed this to Abimelech, he never would have known of God's sovereign protection. Likewise, there have been times when, in God's providence, He prevented what you would have done had He not intervened. You would have committed more failures and sin than you have had God not restrained you. Thus what is written in Scripture:

- "The king's heart is a stream of water in the hand of the Lord; he turns it wherever He will" (Prov. 21:1).
- "And now, behold, I am going to Jerusalem, constrained by the Spirit, not knowing what will happen to me there, except that the Holy Spirit testifies to me in every city that imprisonment and afflictions await me" (Acts 20:22–23).
- "The love of Christ controls us" (2 Cor. 5:14).

While everyone has failed, the number of times God prevented us from sinning against Him is not known. Abimelech was given knowledge of God's intervention, but we most likely will not be given such knowledge until we are in glory, if God chooses to reveal it at all. Still, there is cause to thank God for His grace and mercy in our lives of which we are unaware. Reflect on this for a while, thank God, and then proceed to contemplate personal failure.

How have you failed? Relive your failure(s) for a moment. Know this. You cannot mess up your life, and neither can anyone else, past God being able to restore and use you for His glory. If you don't believe it is a possibility, consider the apostle Peter as a case in point.

Peter denied Jesus once, twice, and then a third time to the point of cursing Him.[319] A denial accompanied by foul language wouldn't have convinced anyone Peter was not a Christ follower. But cursing Jesus accompanied by foul language would have convinced them. Denying and cursing Christ is consistent with Peter's impulsive nature shown previously in trying to decapitate Malchus when Jesus was arrested. [320] Denying Christ and cursing Him would certainly have brought the bitter, weeping Peter experienced afterward.[321] This was a personal failure of colossal proportions, which is hard for us to grasp.

Nothing else is recorded about Peter until after the resurrection. However, imagine what the following days might have been like. He may have equated his failure with that of Judas' to a degree. He probably beat himself up constantly for his denials. Guilt must have overwhelmed him. He probably didn't sleep much. When he did sleep and awoke, his first thought was probably how he blew it spectacularly and publicly. Then overwhelming guilt returned. I wonder how many times each denial replayed in his mind. Every time a rooster crowed, what did he think of? How often did he relive Jesus looking at him as the rooster crowed?[322] Tears of brokenness must have flowed often from the depths of his heart. Indeed, Peter experienced an extreme personal failure with no one to blame but himself. He may have been the first to wonder, "How can I ever be forgiven?"

Whatever your personal failure is, it does not rise to the level of Peter's failure. Your personal failures are not as significant as Peter denying and cursing Jesus face-to-face.

Then came Sunday morning. Then came the empty tomb and the resurrection. Then Peter saw the resurrected Jesus Himself. Then Jesus talked with Peter one morning and was restored.[323]

Recognition of personal failure has a way of either hardening or humbling a person. It hardened Judas[324] and humbled Peter.[325] When Jesus asked Peter, "Do you love me?" (Greek: *agape*), Peter replied, "Yes, you know I love you" (Greek: *phileo*). But no longer did Peter make bold statements of what he would or wouldn't do. He now knew he was unpredictable. Gone were the bold statements of "I will never abandon you!" and "I will die with you!"[326] Now he says, "Lord, you know everything," implying he didn't. Peter was still reeling from his personal failure. Peter had failed, but Jesus would not cast Peter aside.[327]

In the world, after one personal failure, people are often dropped, fired, demoted, or never trusted again. Many times, the individual loses his or her confidence. He or she withdraws, refusing to return to positions of responsibility for fear he or she might fail again. The problem with such an attitude is it is not found in Scripture or in the conduct of Jesus with Peter.

After Peter's personal failure, what does Jesus do? He gives Peter the most significant and important position in the church, to lead, shepherd, teach, and encourage those for whom He died[328] Just as Peter denied Christ three times, Jesus affirmed His love and restoration of Peter three times by asking, "Do you love me?" It could be said it was because of Peter's failure he was qualified by Jesus to fill a preeminent role in the early church. Peter became the shining example of redemption and restoration after personal failure. Proof is given in that it was Peter who denied and cursed Jesus and then preached the inaugural message at Pentecost where God saved three thousand souls, and more were added each day.[329]

At some point, Peter must have remembered Jesus praying for him and the command Jesus tied to the prayer.[330] Jesus told Peter that Satan had asked to "sift (Him) like wheat." In response, Jesus prayed Peter's faith would not fail and after he was restored to strengthen his brothers. From the perspective of the resurrection, Jesus' restoration, the ascension, and Pentecost, Peter must have been greatly encouraged. His personal failure had not disqualified him from the kingdom. Nor did it prevent God from using him again for His glory. Remember, you cannot mess up your life, and neither can anyone else, to the point of God not being able to restore and use you for His glory. Peter is proof.

No matter what happens, what you do or don't do or how much you fail or blow it, there is a reason to be hopeful. The same Jesus who prayed for Peter is praying for you. Not only is Jesus praying for you, the Holy Spirit is as well. These are certain truths because of what is recorded in the Bible.

> Likewise the Spirit helps us in our weakness. For we do not know what to pray for as we ought, but the Spirit himself intercedes for us with groanings too deep for words. And he who searches hearts knows what is the mind of the Spirit, because the Spirit intercedes for the saints according to the will of God ... Who is to condemn? Christ Jesus is the one who died—more than that, who was raised—who is at the right hand of God, who indeed is interceding for us (Rom. 8:26–27, 34).

> [Jesus] is able also to save forever those who draw near to God through him, since he always lives to make intercession for them (Heb. 7:25).

Meditate on these verses. Push them deep into your heart. Believe God, and praise Him!

Redemption from personal failure is the reason Jesus died and was resurrected. He paid the penalty for our personal failures (sin). He satisfied God's wrath toward us and our sin. Thus, Paul wrote in Romans 8:1, "There is therefore now no condemnation for those who are in Christ Jesus."

There's no condemnation for past personal failure(s). There's no condemnation for personal mistakes, accidental blunders, or things we did on purpose that wounded others. There is no condemnation for anything any Christian has ever done, no matter what it may be because the blood of Jesus cleanses from all sin.[331] Because God has forgiven every believer absolutely and completely of all failures (sin), then no one anywhere, regardless of who he or she is, can separate him or her from the love of God that is in Christ Jesus.[332] All sin is forgiven—past, present, and future.

When you fail, regardless of the degree of your failure, remember God is able, can, does, and will restore you according to His great mercy. Again, you cannot mess up your life, and neither can anyone else, past God being able to restore and use you for His glory.

Personal Failure and Restoration

Now I have a word when you have failed and desire restoration. This is included because personal failures affect others, and simply asking them to forgive you is not enough. Personal failure leaves a field of debris that is wide-ranging, long-lasting, and full of deep pain. Let me explain.

David failed by committing adultery and murder.[333] The prophet Nathan confronted him, saying to his face, "You are the man!" Immediately, David repented. He didn't argue or defend himself. Nathan told him that his sin was forgiven; however, the consequences would not be removed and would be: David would be at war the rest of his life, his own family would rebel against Him (Absalom), his wives would be raped publicly, and the child born to Bathsheba would die.[334]

One sinful act left a wake of destruction unimaginable to David at the time. Those affected were God and His reputation,[335] Uriah, the child, the nation of Israel, David's wives along with their parents and children, Absalom, Bathsheba's parents, Uriah's parents, and David himself. After so much devastation due to sin, God could not "just forgive" David and then move on as if nothing ever happened. To do so would not be loving or just.

David was forgiven, but that did not negate the consequences of his sin. Likewise, when we fail personally, God forgives, but the earthly consequences of failure are not removed. God's grace will be sufficient to endure His loving discipline,[336] but the fallout of personal failure is always tragic and far-reaching. Paul was right to pen these words in Galatians 6:7–8, "Do not be deceived: God is not mocked, for whatever one sows, that will he also reap. For the one who sows to his own flesh will from the flesh reap corruption, but the one who sows to the Spirit will from the Spirit reap eternal life."

When we fail personally, God loves us so much that He disciplines us for our good so our soul is saved. He initially does this through his people, the church. Only if ignored does God go further to discipline us Himself. It is better to be disciplined now by our perfect, loving, heavenly Father for a short time (Which means the rest of your life on earth) than to escape discipline now but endure it for eternity separated from Him. Consider what Paul in 1 Corinthians 5:4–5 wrote. "When you are assembled in the name of the Lord Jesus and my spirit is present, with the power of our Lord Jesus, you are to deliver this man to Satan for the destruction of the flesh, so that his spirit may be saved in the day of the Lord."

Saying you're sorry is not a complete apology; nor is it sufficient to restore a relationship that has been damaged, whether the sin perpetrated against another was intended or not. In order for comfort to take place for the wounded party, as well as the one who caused the pain, Scripture must be followed. Thus, Jesus said in Matthew 5:23–24, "If you are offering your gift at the altar and there remember that your brother has something against you, leave your gift there before the altar and go. First be reconciled to your brother, and then come and offer your gift."

One takeaway from this passage is that it isn't possible or acceptable to worship God when there is a problem between one person and another. A personal failure that has wounded another person must be dealt with biblically before God's comfort and blessing will be applied. The same is forcibly set forth in Isaiah 1:12–15 where it is recorded that God says,

> When you come to appear before me, who has required
> of you this trampling of my courts? Bring no more vain

offerings; incense (prayer) is an abomination to me. New moon and Sabbath and the calling of convocations— I cannot endure iniquity and solemn assembly. Your new moons and your appointed feasts my soul hates; they have become a burden to me; I am weary of bearing them. When you spread out your hands, I will hide my eyes from you; even though you make many prayers, I will not listen; your hands are full of blood.

The process of restoration and reconciliation after personal failure is worth examining. Consider from 2 Corinthians 7:10–13 that there is a difference between godly and worldly sorrow. They feel the same (embarrassment and pain), but the result of godly sorrow is vastly different from worldly sorrow.

> Godly grief (sorrow) produces a repentance that leads to salvation without regret, whereas worldly grief (sorrow) produces death. For see what earnestness this godly grief has produced in you, but also what eagerness to clear yourselves, what indignation, what fear, what longing, what zeal, what punishment! At every point you have proved yourselves innocent in the matter. So although I wrote to you, it was not for the sake of the one who did the wrong, nor for the sake of the one who suffered the wrong, but in order that your earnestness for us might be revealed to you in the sight of God. Therefore we are comforted.

Keep your heart sensitive to sin so that, when you fail personally, you will have godly sorrow, repenting from deep inside and doing whatever it takes to make things right.[337] When godly sorrow fills a person, the result is always comfort. Conversely, worldly sorrow is fear of consequences and anger at getting caught that always results in death of relationships, heart, soul, and spirit. Be not deceived. God is not mocked.

When you have failed personally and godly sorrow is working in you, you will naturally want to be serious (earnest) to address and make the situation right. You will be grieved in your soul that you have offended God and man. You will be eager to work toward reconciliation, restoration, and forgiveness through your own personal repentance. You will be angry at yourself (indignation) for the sin you committed. You will have fear that your heart is so sinful as to sin so easily. There will be a strong passion within you (zeal) to address the situation as quickly and fairly as possible. You will be willing to submit yourself to do whatever is necessary to be right with God and those you offended saying, "I deserve whatever I get for my failure" (punishment). You will not rebel against discipline for your failure because you have embraced and understood God's purpose for you and your ultimate good as found in Hebrews 12:4–11.

> In your struggle against sin you have not yet resisted to the point of shedding your blood. And have you forgotten the exhortation that addresses you as sons? "My son, do not regard lightly the discipline of the Lord, nor be weary when reproved by him. For the Lord disciplines the one he loves, and chastises every son whom he receives." It is for discipline that you have to endure. God is treating you as sons. For what son is there whom his father does not discipline? If you are left without discipline, in which all have participated, then you are illegitimate children and not sons. Besides this, we have had earthly fathers who disciplined us and we respected them. Shall we not much more be subject to the Father of spirits and live? For they disciplined us for a short time as it seemed best to them, but he disciplines us for our good, that we may share his holiness. For the moment all discipline seems painful rather than pleasant, but later it yields the peaceful fruit of righteousness to those who have been trained by it.

"Regressive" Sanctification and Personal Failure

Christian maturity is not a steady, only upward growth curve. Instead, Christian growth is an up-and-down proposition. There will be victories, followed by failure, followed by victory, followed by failure, followed by victory, and so forth. Over a lifetime, every genuine Christian's growth trajectory is ultimately positive. The times when we regress in our sanctification are not necessarily cause for anxiety.

There are stretches of time when we mature in Christ. We grow in the disciplines of prayer, worship, Bible reading, evangelism, and so forth. Then we regress in our sanctification each time we sin. Instead of moving forward, we slip, and it has been called backsliding. It's the classic two steps forward and one step back. Or ten steps forward and two steps back throughout life. But those times are not reasons for sorrow.

Backward/forward events happen to the best of God's children, including the heroes of the faith. All believers have mountaintop experiences that are followed by deep valleys of depression or failure. Our lives are like a line on a graph. There are ups and downs, but ultimately, the movement is up toward Christ likeness, godliness, and holiness.

Consider Noah who obeyed God to build the ark and then got drunk after the flood.[338] Abraham followed God's call and then lied about his wife Sarah being his sister.[339] Moses, who led Israel out of bondage, then sinned by striking a rock to bring forth water instead of speaking to it.[340] David was a man after God's own heart but committed adultery and murder.[341] Peter confessed Jesus was the Son of God, denied Christ three times, preached at Pentecost where thousands were saved, and then hypocritically refused to fellowship with Gentile believers.[342] Paul saw heaven and talked to Jesus personally, yet he wrote that he didn't do what he wanted to do but he did what he didn't want to do. The desire for godliness was present in him, but the ability to carry it out wasn't there.[343]

Every Christian fails. We must then repent and confess our sin to God.[344] Personal failure reminds us we trust in God at all times knowing our sanctification is in God's hands and subject to His will.[345] Just because you fail does not mean your faith has failed nor that the One you trust in will abandon you. You will have great times of fellowship with God and growth in Christ, but don't be surprised when you fail momentarily. Confess your sin and continue following Christ. It is those who keep on following Christ, in spite of their failures, who are genuinely saved.[346]

Sanctification's Trajectory Is Ultimately Positive[347]

No one event defines you or your faith in Christ. The determining element of your faith is over the course of a lifetime. Overall, in and through everything, every genuine Christian will grow and mature in Christ, even when, in his or her view, he or she regresses in his or her faith. It is the overall trajectory of becoming more like Jesus that God will make happen without any possibility of failure.[348]

Here is a description of the overall upward trajectory that Christians experience over a lifetime: salvation and receiving spiritual gifts from God, which are applied according to His will.[349] As with salvation,[350] everyone's level of maturity attained in Christ is in God's hands.[351] Believers are to work to grow in the gifts and grace given by God.[352] Thus, 2 Peter 1:5–8 says,

> For this very reason, make every effort to supplement your faith with virtue, and virtue with knowledge, and knowledge with self-control, and self-control with steadfastness, and steadfastness with godliness, and godliness with brotherly affection, and brotherly affection with love. For if these qualities are yours and are increasing, they keep you from being ineffective or unfruitful in the knowledge of our Lord Jesus Christ.

The forward and backward, up and down, and growth and regression (personal failure) in the Christian life does not happen randomly. They are the result of God's determination along with personal activity to grow in Christ. Because all are sinners, failures shouldn't be surprising. When they happen, repent of the failure, submit the area of failure anew to Christ, and keep pressing on toward the upward call in Christ.[353]

For Serious Contemplation: Whether Or Not Salvation Is Genuine

There is a difference between the normal ups and downs of life (personal failures) with an overall upward trajectory of a Christian maturity and one that "(has) the appearance of godliness but (denies) its power."[354] The second describes a life that is not redeemed. Being assured of salvation is essential for every believer, and everything written about in *Dancing in the Dungeon* includes those who are in vocational ministry.[355]

Conduct is a product of the heart. As it is written, "Out of the abundance of the heart the mouth speaks,"[356] it is just as true that conduct is a product of the heart. Someone wrote that thoughts produce words produce conduct produces character and results in destiny. This is true. So what does your heart desire? What do you think about when you have nothing else to think about? What conduct can you trace back to words and thoughts that reveal the condition of your heart? Is it possible that you know about Christ but He does not know you?[357]

Paul writes something interesting to the church at Corinth because a number of issues gave the apostle reason to call them to examine their faith as to whether or not they were genuinely saved. 2 Corinthians 13:5 says, "Examine yourselves, to see whether you are in the faith. Test yourselves. Or do you not realize this about yourselves, that Jesus Christ is in you?—unless indeed you fail to meet the test!"

As Paul observed their behavior, it seemed the trajectory of their conduct was not toward God but away from Him. Some of the events He (metaphorically speaking) put on a graph included:

- There was division among them as a fellowship.[358]
- This included division based on perceived spiritual maturity.[359]
- They argued who should lead the church.[360]
- In some way, they weren't taking care of their physical bodies.[361]
- They were arrogant toward one another instead of gracious and loving.[362]
- They accepted, approved, and boasted about scandalous immorality in their midst.[363]
- They refused to implement loving discipline.[364]
- Their divisions were so deep that they were suing each other in court.[365]
- There was significant sexual immorality in the church.[366]
- Marriage, divorce, and remarriage were grossly misunderstood.[367]
- By their conduct, they caused other believers to stumble in their faith.[368]
- Because of their conduct, some were weak and sick, and some had died.[369]

Those are a few reasons Paul questioned the genuine nature of their conversion. The trajectory of their life was not maturing in Christ but rather seemed to give evidence of false conversions.[370] Similarly, it is wise for every person, believers included, to periodically examine his or her life trajectory from the heart. What a tragedy it will be for those who were given the chance to repent and refused to because they thought they were saved, only to have Jesus reject them on judgment day.[371] Consider the Scripture.

- "For God so loved the world, that he gave his only Son, that whoever believes in Him should not perish but have eternal life. For God did not send his Son into the world to condemn the world, but in order that the world might be saved through him" (John 3:16–17).
- "If you confess with your mouth that Jesus is Lord and believe in your heart that God raised Him from the dead, you will be saved. For with the heart one believes and is justified, and with the mouth one confesses and is saved. For the Scripture says, 'Everyone who believes in Him will not be put to shame'" (Rom. 10:9–11).
- "If we confess our sins, he is faithful and just to forgive us our sins and to cleanse us from all unrighteousness" (1 John 1:9).
- "Believe in the Lord Jesus, and you will be saved" (Acts 16:31).
- "Let all the house of Israel therefore know for certain that God has made Him both Lord and Christ, this Jesus whom you crucified. Now when they heard this they were cut to the heart, and said to Peter and the rest of the apostles, 'Brothers, what shall we do?' And Peter said to them, 'Repent and be baptized every one of you in the name of Jesus Christ for the forgiveness of your sins, and you will receive the gift of the Holy Spirit. For the promise is for you and for your children and for all who are far off, everyone whom the Lord our God calls to himself'" (Acts 2:36–40).

Confirm your salvation in Christ by examining your heart and the overall trajectory of your life. Test yourself to see if you are in the faith because Christ is in you, unless you fail the test.

Discussion Questions

- Discuss God preventing you from failing personally.
- What do you think about no one being able to mess up your life past God using for His glory? Explain.
- What do you think of forgiveness for failure not negating consequences (David)?
- Discuss the meaning of 1 Corinthians 5:4–5.
- Discuss the difference between worldly and godly grief (repentance) from 2 Corinthians 7:10–13.

Reflection #9: Truth Trumps Feelings

I was so emotionally down that I had pretty much stayed in bed over a week. Most of that time was spent looking at the ceiling or staring into a corner asking myself, "Have you just royally screwed up again?" I followed that up with, "Yes, you have. And you can't change it. Just accept you have failed and you are a failure. Everyone knows it. Accept it yourself." Amazingly, I had attained absolute omniscience. I knew the future like the prophets of old. In reality, my omniscience was assumed, not genuine.

Of course, two of the previous sentences are false, but that's the way people think when life beats them down more than once. When "assumed omniscience" takes root in a person's mind, it can be crippling and lead to depression. It is, at best, false. At worse, it's a heinous sin and certainly arrogance of heart remembering what is written in James 4:14–15, "You do not know what tomorrow will bring... You ought to say, 'If the Lord wills, we will live and do this or that.'"

David had been chosen by God and anointed to be king. That meant, by God's power, he would be king. But then King Saul sought to kill him. David forgot his call and anointing by focusing on his misperceived circumstances. We know this because of what is written in 2 Samuel 27:1, "David said in his heart, I shall now perish one day by the hand of Saul." C.H. Spurgeon wrote about this verse,

> David could not put his finger upon any entry in his diary, and say of it, "Here is evidence that the Lord will forsake me," for the entire tenor of his past life proved the very reverse. He should have argued from what God had done for him, that God would be his defender still. But is it not just in the same way that we doubt God's help? Is it not mistrust without a cause? Have we ever had the shadow of a reason to doubt our Father's goodness? Have not his loving kindnesses been marvelous? Has he once failed to justify our trust? Let us not, then, reason

contrary to evidence. How can we ever be so ungenerous as to doubt our God? Lord, throw down the Jezebel of our unbelief, and let the dogs devour it.[372]

As many have said, we don't know what tomorrow holds, but we do know God holds tomorrow in His hand. And so I have found the way to overcome assumed omniscience is to reflect instead on the truth of God's Word. Then I find myself following God through the darkness. Consider the phrases below for meditation:

- "Fear not, for I am with you; be not dismayed, for I am your God; I will strengthen you, I will help you, I will uphold you with my righteous right hand."[373]
- "[God] has said, 'I will never leave you nor forsake you.'"[374]
- "'Why are you afraid, O you of little faith?' Then (Jesus) rose and rebuked the winds and the sea, and there was a great calm."[375]
- "Fear not, therefore; you are of more value than many sparrows."[376]
- "When the disciples saw [Jesus] walking on the sea they said, 'It is a ghost!' and they cried out in fear. But… Jesus said, 'Take heart; it is I. Do not be afraid.'"[377]
- "Fear not, little flock, for it is your Father's good pleasure to give you the kingdom. Sell your possessions, and give to the needy. Where your treasure is, there will your heart be also."[378]
- "Do not be afraid, but go on speaking and do not be silent, for I am with you, and no one will attack you to harm you, for I have many in this city who are my people."[379]

CHAPTER 10

WHEN SHEEP ATTACK SHEPHERDS

Note: This chapter is primarily for ministers, and it is written in a format that ministers are used to, from one who has walked through difficult days in ministry. Those not in ministry will be able to find encouragement; however, the focus is aimed at those who are in vocational ministry and are struggling spiritually and emotionally, possibly to the point of having to resign their position.

If God's people are to dance when they are in a dungeon of adversity, they must have learned to do so by observing their shepherd dance in their own dungeon of adversity. Of course, God uses the messages and studies what the minister presents to a congregation, but those are useless if not backed up by the minister's conduct when he is in difficulty. There was a reason why, when Paul was in prison, he wrote Philippians 4:8–9.

> Finally, brothers, whatever is true, whatever is honorable, whatever is just, whatever is pure, whatever is lovely, whatever is commendable, if there is any excellence, if there is anything worthy of praise, think about these things. What you have learned and received and heard and seen in me—practice these things, and the God of peace will be with you.

Yes, Paul was chained between two guards twenty-four hours a day, but he was at peace. Yes, there was the possibility of being killed,[380] but he was at peace. Yes, people tried to add insult to injury while Paul was incarcerated,[381] but he was at peace. Paul's faith was such that he was content whatever circumstance he was in.[382] It is not an accident that the suffering God willed into Paul's life[383] resulted in other believers' boldness to proclaim the gospel in the face of possible arrest and/or execution.[384] When ministers are the example of joyfully suffering for God's glory, then God's people are emboldened to also glorify God in whatever circumstances they find themselves in. Suffering joyfully for God's glory gives the gospel and those who proclaim it credibility that proclamation alone does not provide.

Originally, this book was intended for pastors, but they are not the only ones who struggle. So do other ministers. Thus, the scope was broadened to include all ministers. But ministers are not the only ones who suffer. All Christians suffer according to God's will.[385] Therefore, the book has been written for all believers who need help and encouragement to joyfully suffer in a manner that glorifies God and led to the title, *Dancing in the Dungeon*. This chapter is written to suggest to ministers a few encouragements that God used to comfort me in the context of vocational ministry.

From One Minister to Another

When I struggled in ministry, I wanted to hear from someone who had suffered like me. I gave little credence to those who spoke from an ivory tower of education but had no scars. Those who had walked a similar path to mine, with scars to prove it, were the ones I wanted to hear. Missionary Amy Carmichael wrote about the necessity of trials that result in scars.

> Have you no scar? No scar that is hidden? I hear people talk of how great you are. They say you are like a star

in the heavens! But don't you have a scar? Haven't you been wounded for Christ? Many are the wounds of the faithful. Archers have used them for target practice. They feel like dying under a tree, surrounded by wild animals, about to expire. So where is your wound? Don't you have one? Yes, as the Master is, so shall his servant be. Pierced are the hands and feet that follow him. But yours are whole! Can anyone have followed Him far… who has no wound or scar?

Difficulties in ministry are no different from anyone else's. Suffering people don't appreciate a minister bemoaning how hard life is because they live in a "dog eat dog" world more vicious than the one the minister lives in. The difference between ministers and others is not that suffering happens, but the context in which suffering takes place. For a minister, it is usually in a local congregation. Another difference is an expectation of unbelievers inflicting pain, but it should not be so in the church where everyone is called to be loving, forgiving, merciful, and gracious to one another. Yet sadly, this is the case too often.

So the minister reading this will know that I have had difficulties much like his or hers. I offered events from twenty-three years as a pastor in the foreword. My reason is so ministers will know we may have like experiences, and God provides comfort in them.

God blessed congregations I served with growth, buildings, elimination of debt, vision for the future, and many dear Christian friends who are precious to my family and me. While there were difficult days, my experience is that God is the God of comfort, as Paul wrote in 2 Corinthians 1:3–7.

> Blessed be the God and Father of our Lord Jesus Christ, the Father of mercies and God of all comfort, who comforts us in all our affliction, so that we may be able to comfort those who are in any affliction, with the comfort with which we ourselves are comforted by

God. For as we share abundantly in Christ's sufferings, so through Christ we share abundantly in comfort too. If we are afflicted, it is for your comfort and salvation; and if we are comforted, it is for your comfort, which you experience when you patiently endure the same sufferings that we suffer. Our hope for you is unshaken, for we know that as you share in our sufferings, you will also share in our comfort.

What now follows is a process formulated over time that God used to comfort me in my afflictions. My prayer is for those in ministry to mull over these things as Paul encouraged Timothy to do while relying on God, "Think over what I say, for the Lord will give you understanding in everything."[386]

The Process for Being Comforted by God

These are "comfort(s) by which I have been comforted by God" during the darkest and most difficult days of my life and ministry. I have worked through what follows many times in the course of decades and found God to be faithful to comfort me every time. No matter how dark the day, the severity of the struggle, or how hopeless you feel, God can and will encourage, strengthen, and establish you.[387] The following reflections are the way He did those things in my life. May He do the same for you to His glory. Work through what follows slowly, prayerfully, and honestly by trusting God.

An Important Personal Word and Suggestion

On January 15, 2013, from 7:30 a.m. to 12:45 p.m., God broke and comforted me as I'd never before experienced. I was hurting, confused, scared, and angry all at the same time because a personnel team had asked me to resign in opposition to the deacon leadership the previous November, which I decided to do. Then a month later, on a personal level, I had the rug pulled from under me three times in ten days. Now I wasn't sure if I had done the right thing but rather made a colossal mistake. In the midst of this dark day, I downloaded a song from Together 4 the Gospel (T4G), "I Asked the Lord That I Might Grow" by John Newton. As I listened to the song while reading the words, I broke down in weeping and brokenness, not for my mistake but for misunderstanding God's love in the midst of hurt and pain.

My suggestion is for the reader to go to You Tube[388] and search for "T4G I Asked the Lord That I Might Grow." Listen to the song while you read the lyrics I've included in Appendix A.

Ministerial Conduct in the Process Of Termination

Nothing tests our obedience to Christ like conflict.[389] Dear fellow ministers of the gospel, I have been in countless difficult church situations. There aren't many things you are, have, or will go through that I have not already endured. More than once, I've had letters of resignation placed before me to sign. I've been surprised by groups from five to twenty pressuring me and calling for my resignation.[390] Meetings I was not invited to have taken place to discuss my future. I know the hurt, fear, and disappointment that goes along with being placed in uncomfortable situations without having an advocate. I have wept after these meetings not knowing what to tell my wife and family. I have most likely walked in your shoes. (Read the foreword.)

Each time, I had to decide how I would respond and conduct myself. While I confess to making mistakes along the way, I can say that God honors those who honor Him. So I ask you to seriously consider what I suggest here for God to work in you for His glory.[391]

It is written in Hebrews 13:17 that you will give an account to the Father for your conduct as one who is held to a higher standard.[392] Remember that Jesus died to save those who believe and He takes how they are treated seriously.[393] The church is the bride of Christ, and as such, it is always to be treated with the utmost respect and dignity. The most important message you will ever deliver to a congregation is how you conduct yourself in the midst of pressure, adversity, and trial when your future at the church is in doubt. Therefore, I present for your consideration things to do and not do. Please meditate on each of them prayerfully and seriously.

- DO continue to preach and serve faithfully without taking shots at anyone.
- DO be gracious and kind to everyone.
- DO answer questions posed to you honestly with an attitude of mercy and grace.[394]
- DO trust God who is in complete control of all things.[395]
- DO pray for (not against) those who oppose you, asking God to bless them.[396]
- DO examine your own life and heart, repenting of all sin.[397]
- DO forgive quickly, totally, and completely whether people ask or not.[398]
- Do NOT wage a rumor campaign against your adversaries.
- Do NOT say things publicly that harm other believers, regardless of who they are or what they have said or done.
- Do NOT say anything from the pulpit in a mean-spirited or vindictive manner ever.
- Do NOT be combative, argumentative, or bitter in committee or team meetings.
- DO meditate long and deep on the following scriptures:
- "Do not resist the one who is evil. But if anyone slaps you on the right cheek, turn to Him the other also. And if anyone would sue you and take your tunic, let Him have your cloak as well. And if anyone forces you to go one mile, go with Him two miles" (Matt. 5:39–41).
- "If anyone will not receive you or listen to your words, shake off the dust from your feet when you leave that house or town. Truly, I say to you, it will be more bearable on the day

of judgment for the land of Sodom and Gomorrah than for that town" (Matt. 10:14–15).
- "When they persecute you in one town, flee to the next" (Matt. 10:23).
- "Let love be genuine. Love one another with brotherly affection. Outdo one another in showing honor ... Be patient in tribulation, be constant in prayer ... Bless those who persecute you; bless and do not curse them ... Repay no one evil for evil, but give thought to do what is honorable in the sight of all. If possible, so far as it depends on you, live peaceably with all. Beloved, never avenge yourselves, but leave it to the wrath of God. To the contrary, if your enemy is hungry, feed him; if he is thirsty, give Him something to drink; Do not be overcome by evil, but overcome evil with good" (Rom. 12:9–10, 12, 14, 17–21).
- "Let all bitterness and wrath and anger and clamor and slander be put away from you, along with all malice. Be kind to one another, tenderhearted, forgiving one another, as God in Christ forgave you" (Eph. 4:31–32).
- "Whatever happens, conduct yourselves in a manner worthy of the gospel of Christ" (Phil. 1:27) (NIV).
- "If when you do good and suffer for it you endure, this is a gracious thing in the sight of God. For to this you have been called, because Christ also suffered for you, leaving you an example, so that you might follow in his steps. He committed no sin, neither was deceit found in his mouth. When he was reviled, he did not revile in return; when he suffered, he did not threaten, but continued entrusting himself to Him who judges justly. He himself bore our sins in his body on the tree, that we might die to sin and live to righteousness. By his wounds you have been healed" (1 Peter 2:20–24).

I know your inclination is to fight back, but that is contrary to turning the other cheek and how Jesus conducted Himself when in the religious context He was attacked (1 Peter above). Remember also how Stephen conducted himself when hauled before the Sanhedrin and spoke winsomely.[399] When you are persecuted for doing good, you are in good company, and great is your reward in heaven.[400] You are not living for this world's evaluation[401] but to one day hear Jesus say, "Well done, good and faithful servant."[402] Now I will describe the comforts by which I have been comforted by God.

Settle Your Conversion to Christ

I rely on the bedrock affirmation daily that I am saved by the blood of Jesus and my name is in the Book of Life. This truth informs and drives everything I think and do. Because I'm saved, there are other things I believe to the depths of my soul, which will be found below. Settling your conversion is important because my dad was an alcoholic pastor but not a believer. He led people to Christ, preached the gospel, and taught God's Word diligently, but he was not saved. Six weeks before he died, he was hopefully converted. It is entirely possible to be a minister of the gospel and not a genuine believer in Christ.

Judas Iscariot was an apostle for three years. He preached the gospel, cast out demons, and healed people in the name of Jesus, but he was not saved.[403] In 1687, Elias Keach was asked to preach in Philadelphia because his father was a well-known Baptist minister in London. He chose to preach one of his dad's sermons. At one point, he stopped and confessed, "I'm not a preacher or a Christian." He was converted that night and went on to pastor one of the first Baptist churches to survive in America.[404]

Suggesting a person revisit and settle his or her conversion is not new. Paul did such when he wrote his second letter to the Corinthians.[405] Genuine believers never take it as an offense to be asked about their conversion. They are happy and glad to recount how God brought them from darkness to light. They are clear on how and when God converted them. They joyfully recount the event much like Paul did.[406] Only when the assurance of salvation is settled will the following reflections apply.

Settle Your Call to Vocational Ministry

Given the above, not everyone is called by God to ministry. Likewise, not every believer is called by God to vocational ministry.[407] If you are not sure of God's call to vocational ministry, you would do better to be a godly church member than try to do what you haven't been called by God to do in His church. By affirming God's call on your life, you will find strength to persevere.

How does a person confirm God's call? Get alone with God, and honestly evaluate a few things. (You are the only one who can do this under God's leadership.)

1. Reexamine how you knew and believed God first called you to vocational ministry.
2. Are you gifted by God to carry out his call to vocational ministry?
3. Do you have a passion and love deep in your heart for vocational ministry?
4. Do you find great joy in vocational ministry?
5. Is your character consistent with 1 Timothy 3:1–7 and Titus 1:6–9?
6. Is your attitude toward ministry, congregations, staff, and church one of deep love?
7. Do you long for and wish there was something else you could do to pay your bills? Is there anything else you can do and be in God's will? (If the answers to these two questions are yes, in all likelihood, you are not called by God.)

How you answer these questions will either affirm your call or reveal you aren't called. If you are called by God to shepherd his people, persevere! If you aren't called by God, it is better to find another vocation and live for God's glory in it (which is just as high a calling). If God has called you to preach, stay at it. If God has called you to another expression of ministry, follow it.

Fine-Tune Your Theology of Suffering

This section is written for ministers who are used to reading and thinking through propositions with supporting texts. Each point begins with a truth statement followed by an affirmation and the author's personal application, and then it concludes with scripture from which each is based. Keep in mind what is presented below is the author's process of thinking, which has affirmed and comforted him.

As a suggestion, take time to slowly read and reflect on the following truths.[408] Drive them deep into your heart through prayer. As you do this, the Spirit will comfort and strengthen you. The author came to these conclusions for himself and asks the reader to consider them in his or her own context.

Once your conversion and God's call on your life are confirmed, push God's truth regarding suffering that follows deep into your soul. Make them bedrock assertions to embrace, no matter what happens what you feel, regardless of what anyone else says or does. The reason is because what you believe about God is the most important thing about you and informs how you process life events.

Note: It is of great importance that each of the Scripture passages be read with careful meditation and prayer. Apart from prayer and Scripture, I would not have been comforted by God. The reader will notice that each truth is written in a personal manner and are from my personal reflections as I worked out my own theology of suffering. It is assumed ministers will have the tools and discipline necessary to not need overt direction in applying what follows.

Truth 1: Everything Is for God's Glory

Therefore, everything God causes or allows is first and ultimately for His glory.

Personal Application
As I strive toward the goal of glorifying God in everything, I am able to rejoice in God being glorified in and through my personal circumstances.

- "I am the Lord; that is my name; My glory I give to no other, nor my praise to carved idols" (Isa. 42:8).
- "For my own sake, for my own sake, I do it, for how should my name be profaned? My glory I will not give to another" (Isa. 48:11).
- "Now is my soul troubled. And what shall I say? 'Father, save me from this hour'? But for this purpose I have come to this hour. Father, glorify your name. Then a voice came from heaven: 'I have glorified it, and I will glorify it again'" (John 12:27–28).
- "The heavens declare the glory of God, and the sky above proclaims his handiwork. Day to day pours out speech, and night to night reveals knowledge. There is no speech, nor are there words, whose voice is not heard" (Ps. 19:1–3).
- "Be exalted, O God, above the heavens! Let your glory be over all the earth!" (Ps. 57:5).
- "Help us, O God of our salvation, for the glory of your name; deliver us, and atone for our sins, for your name's sake!" (Ps. 79:9).
- "Be exalted, O God, above the heavens! Let your glory be over all the earth!" (Ps. 108:5).

- "Not to us, O Lord, not to us, but to your name give glory, for the sake of your steadfast love and your faithfulness!" (Ps. 115:1).

Truth 2: God Loves Me, and This Truth Will Never Change

Therefore, everything that happens to me comes from God who loves me.

Personal Application

It has been said that just because we don't see how something can be good doesn't mean it isn't good. Complete understanding of a situation, event, or God himself is not required to live by faith while trusting God.

- "What then shall we say to these things? If God is for us, who can be against us? He who did not spare his own Son but gave Him up for us all, how will he not also with Him graciously give us all things? Who shall bring any charge against God's elect? It is God who justifies. Who is to condemn? Christ Jesus is the one who died… more than that, who was raised… who is at the right hand of God, who indeed is interceding for us. Who shall separate us from the love of Christ? Shall tribulation, or distress, or persecution, or famine, or nakedness, or danger, or sword? As it is written, 'For your sake we are being killed all the daylong; we are regarded as sheep to be slaughtered.' No, in all these things we are more than conquerors through Him who loved us. For I am sure that neither death nor life, nor angels nor rulers, nor things present nor things to come, nor powers, nor height nor depth, nor anything else in all creation, will be able to separate us from the love of God in Christ Jesus our Lord" (Rom. 8:31–39).

- "So we have come to know and to believe the love that God has for us. God is love, and whoever abides in love abides in God, and God abides in him" (1 John 4:16).
- "Ask, and it will be given to you; seek, and you will find; knock, and it will be opened to you. For everyone who asks receives, and the one who seeks finds, and to the one who knocks it will be opened. Or which one of you, if his son asks Him for bread, will give Him a stone? Or if he asks for a fish, will give Him a serpent? If you then, who are evil, know how to give good gifts to your children, how much more will your Father who is in heaven give good things to those who ask him!" (Matt. 7:7–11).
- "For God so loved the world, that he gave his only Son, that whoever believes in Him should not perish but have eternal life" (John 3:16).
- "Every good gift and every perfect gift is from above, coming down from the Father of lights with whom there is no variation or shadow due to change" (James 1:17).

Truth 3: Everything Is for Your Ultimate Eternal Good

Therefore, because God is my ultimate good, everything is working to conform me to the image of Christ, which results in holiness and godliness, which glorifies God.

Personal Application
I am able to rejoice in all things knowing what God will accomplish.

- "I am sure of this, that he who began a good work in you <u>will</u> bring it to completion at the day of Jesus Christ" (Phil. 1:6).
- "For it is God who works in you, both to will and to work for his good pleasure" (Phil. 2:13).

- "And we know that God causes all things to work together for good to those who love God, to those who are called according to his purpose. For those whom he foreknew, he also predestined to become conformed to the image of his Son" (Rom. 8:28–29) (NASU).
- "Count it all joy, my brothers, when you meet trials of various kinds, for you know that the testing of your faith produces steadfastness. And let steadfastness have its full effect, that you may be perfect and complete, lacking in nothing" (James 1:2–4).

Truth 4: God Is in Control of You, Your Circumstances, Everyone Else, and All Life Events

Therefore, there is no need to worry or be anxious because the one who loves me is in control, sovereign, and providential in all things. See number three above.

Personal Application

All I can do is all I can do, and all I can do is enough.[409] Therefore, I will rest in Christ, His sovereignty and providence.

- "Remember the former things of old; for I am God, and there is no other; I am God, and there is none like me, declaring the end from the beginning and from ancient times things not yet done, saying, 'My counsel shall stand, and I will accomplish all my purpose'" (Isa. 46:9–10).
- "For his dominion is an everlasting dominion, and his kingdom endures from generation to generation; all the inhabitants of the earth are accounted as nothing, and he does according to His will among the host of heaven and among the inhabitants of the earth; and none can stay his hand or say to Him, 'What have you done?'" (Daniel 4:34–35).

- "For (God) says to Moses, 'I will have mercy on whom I have mercy, and I will have compassion on whom I have compassion.' So then it depends not on human will or exertion, but on God, who has mercy. For the Scripture says to Pharaoh, 'For this very purpose I have raised you up, that I might show my power in you, and that my name might be proclaimed in all the earth.' So then he has mercy on whomever he wills, and he hardens whomever he wills. You will say to me then, 'Why does he still find fault? For who can resist His will?' But who are you, O man, to answer back to God? Will what is molded say to its molder, 'Why have you made me like this?' Has the potter no right over the clay, to make out of the same lump one vessel for honored use and another for dishonorable use?" (Rom. 9:15–21).
- "Rejoice in the Lord always; again I will say, Rejoice. Let your reasonableness be known to everyone. The Lord is at hand; do not be anxious about anything, but in everything by prayer and supplication with thanksgiving let your requests be made known to God" (Phil. 4:4–6).

Truth 5: Trust God Unconditionally

Therefore, God knows better than me what is best, proper, right, and needed. Therefore, I will not worry about God getting it right. He always does.

Personal Application
I can live my life in God's Sabbath rest.

- "Come to me, all who labor and are heavy laden, and I will give you rest. Take my yoke upon you, and learn from me, for I am gentle and lowly in heart, and you will find rest for your souls. For my yoke is easy, and my burden is light" (Matt. 11:28–30).

- "Trust in the Lord with all your heart, and do not lean on your own understanding" (Prov. 3:5).
- "Now faith is the assurance of things hoped for, the conviction of things not seen. For by it the people of old received their commendation" (Heb. 11:1–2).
- "So then, there remains a Sabbath rest for the people of God, for whoever has entered God's rest has also rested from his works as God did from his" (Heb. 4:9–10).

Truth 6: Satan Can Only Do What God Allows (See Numbers One through Five Above)

Therefore, do not fear Satan at any time over anything (1 John 4:4–B).

Personal Application
God uses Satan to bring about my sanctification and His perfect will (Job 1–2).

- "For he who is in you is greater than he who is in the world" (1 John 4:4).

Truth 7: Expect Hardship as God's Call to Increase My Joy and Rewards

Therefore, I can rejoice in this life knowing what awaits me.[410]

Personal Application
Live to hear God say, "Well done, good and faithful servant!"[411]

- "Blessed are those who are persecuted for righteousness' sake, for theirs is the kingdom of heaven. Blessed are you when others revile you and persecute you and utter all kinds of evil against you falsely on my account. Rejoice and be glad, for your reward is great in heaven, for so they persecuted the prophets who were before you" (Matt. 5:10–12).

- "Remember the word that I said to you: 'A servant is not greater than his master.' If they persecuted me, they will also persecute you" (John 15:20).
- "The Spirit himself bears witness with our spirit that we are children of God, and if children, then heirs—heirs of God and fellow heirs with Christ, provided we suffer with Him in order that we may also be glorified with him. For I consider that the sufferings of this present time are not worth comparing with the glory that is to be revealed to us" (Rom. 8:16–18).
- "But he said to me, 'My grace is sufficient for you, for my power is made perfect in weakness.' Therefore I will boast all the more gladly of my weaknesses, so that the power of Christ may rest upon me. For the sake of Christ, then, I am content with weaknesses, insults, hardships, persecutions, and calamities. For when I am weak, then I am strong" (2 Cor. 12:9–10).
- "For it has been granted to you that for the sake of Christ you should not only believe in Him but also suffer for his sake" (Phil. 1:29).
- "Beloved, do not be surprised at the fiery trial when it comes upon you to test you, as though something strange were happening to you. But rejoice insofar as you share Christ's sufferings, that you may also rejoice and be glad when His glory is revealed. If you are insulted for the name of Christ, you are blessed, because the Spirit of glory and of God rests upon you" (1 Peter 4:12–15).
- "For this is a gracious thing, when, mindful of God, one endures sorrows while suffering unjustly. For what credit is it if, when you sin and are beaten for it, you endure? But if when you do good and suffer for it you endure, this is a gracious thing in the sight of God. For to this you have

been called, because Christ also suffered for you, leaving you an example, so that you might follow in his steps" (1 Peter 2:19–21).

Seriously Consider God's Loving Discipline

Types of Discipline
Formative and corrective

Scripture

Formative Discipline: "To keep me from being too elated by the surpassing greatness of the revelations, a thorn was given me in the flesh, a messenger of Satan to harass me, to keep me from being too elated" (2 Cor. 12:7).

Corrective Discipline: "Consider Him who endured from sinners such hostility against himself, so that you may not grow weary or fainthearted. In your struggle against sin you have not yet resisted to the point of shedding your blood. And have you forgotten the exhortation that addresses you as sons? 'My son, do not regard lightly the discipline of the Lord, nor be weary when reproved by him. For the Lord disciplines the one he loves, and chastises every son whom he receives.' It is for discipline that you have to endure. God is treating you as sons. For what son is there whom his father does not discipline? If you are left without discipline… then you are illegitimate children and not sons. Besides this, we have had earthly fathers who disciplined us and we respected them. Shall we not much more be subject to the Father of spirits and live? For they disciplined us for a short time as it seemed best to them, but he disciplines us for our good, that we may share his holiness. For the moment all discipline seems painful rather than pleasant, but later it yields the peaceful fruit of righteousness to those who have been trained by it. Therefore lift your drooping hands and strengthen your weak knees (Heb. 12:3–12).

Definition

Formative protects; corrective reproves. God's love motivates both.

Results

Holiness, godliness, Christ likeness, peace, joy, and rewards[412]

Discerning the Difference
- "Ask, and it will be given to you; seek, and you will find; knock, and it will be opened to you. For everyone who asks receives, and the one who seeks finds, and to the one who knocks it will be opened. Or which one of you, if his son asks Him for bread, will give Him a stone? Or if he asks for a fish, will give Him a serpent? If you then, who are evil, know how to give good gifts to your children, how much more will your Father who is in heaven give good things to those who ask him!" (Matt. 7:7–11).
- "If any of you lacks wisdom, let Him ask God, who gives generously to all without reproach, and it will be given him. But let Him ask in faith, with no doubting, for the one who doubts is like a wave of the sea that is driven and tossed by the wind. For that person must not suppose that he will receive anything from the Lord" (James 1:5–7).

Application

Through prayer, I seek to discern what God is doing in my life and (to the best of my ability) why He is doing it. Ask for insight and help from people who are wiser and godlier than you are.

Truth

God is never angry in discipline. All of God's anger and wrath toward me was imputed to Jesus on the cross. Therefore, God is not angry with you. Thus, what you are going through must be an expression of His love for your good and His glory. God's Spirit will reveal His purpose to you as you seek God on this point.

Conclusion

The process above requires honest evaluation and spiritual discipline before God. My experience is that, over time, the insights God grants result in tremendous joy, peace, and contentment. I ask that you consider that there are times in our life God that sends us to Egypt (Joseph in Genesis), the backside of Midian (Moses), and the desert of Arabia (Paul) in order to get our attention, discipline us for our good, and prepare us for the future He has planned. Our responsibility is to work with God and be clay in His hands.

Ministers must dance in the dungeon because God's people look to them as examples to follow.[413] When they observe their ministers suffering in a joyful manner for God's glory, that makes a stronger statement to the validity of God's Word and power than many sermons. For ministers not to suffer in a manner that glorifies God, the gospel is invalidated.[414] The difficulties I encountered in ministry most helped me to formulate my theology of suffering, which I present again for consideration and reflection.

> Every hurt, disappointment, and pain in life is placed there by a loving God who wills only the absolute best for His own, now and forever.[415] God's goal is not so much ease and comfort in this life as it is His glory[416] and the strength of His children's faith.[417] God never allows anything into His children's lives that is anything but good in His all wise knowledge.[418] God is so determined to make His children like His Son that He does not leave it to chance, but He wills it without any possibility of failure.[419] Therefore, everything the Christian experiences is ultimately good, increases joy, lays up treasure in heaven, and is to be understood in these contexts.[420]

Discussion Questions

- If you are not a minister, what do you think of what is written in this chapter?
- How is a minister's life different from your own, or is it different?
- What do you think of the process the author suggests for ministers to follow?
- Did any of the truths illicit an unexpected response or thoughts? Which ones and why?

Ron Ethridge Jr.

Reflection #10: Answering the Hardest Question... Why?

Eventually, the question "Why?" is asked when difficult times hit anyone. Among many possible answers (see chapter 4), there is another answer for when the most difficult of events enter life, that is, when a loved one unexpectedly loses his or her life.

Early in my ministry, a young man of eighteen died unexpectedly during the night. He had just started getting his life in order from drugs and alcohol. He was attending college while living at home with his mother. Life was finally turning around for him. When his mother went in to wake him up for class one morning, he was unresponsive. The medical team called to the scene declared him dead.

When I arrived, the mother was understandably devastated. In the midst of her deep sorrow, she looked me in the eye and asked, "Why would God do this to my son?" I didn't have an answer, but I knew I had to give her some kind of response that included hope. I prayed with her and went back to my study, asking God to give me something to encourage her and those who would be at the funeral.

At some point in my study and searching Scripture, I came upon Isaiah 57:1–2. "The righteous man perishes, and no one lays it to heart; devout men are taken away, while no one understands. For the righteous man is taken away from calamity; he enters into peace; they rest in their beds."

Upon reflection and prayer, I came to understand that the all wise and loving God's thoughts are not our thoughts. Nor are His ways our ways.[421] Thus, there are times it could be (note those last three words) that God decides to bring one of His children home to spare him or her greater suffering had he or she continued to live in a broken world. Had he or she lived longer on earth, he or she may have experienced great heartache, suffering, and hardship, and so in His wisdom and love, He decides to spare him or her the pain he or she would have experienced by bringing him or her to his or her eternal home in His presence.

Indeed, "God causes all things to work together for the good of those who love Him, who are the called according to His purpose."[422] "Just because we don't see how something can be good doesn't mean it isn't good."[423] As someone has said, "Don't doubt in the dark what God has revealed to you in the light." This includes what we perceive to be tragedies, disasters, and calamities. It is best to take God at His Word and believe Him no matter what we think, feel, or desire at the time. Thus, when life doesn't make sense, I choose to reflect on the following passages:

- "Trust in the Lord with all your heart, and do not lean on your own understanding" (Prov. 3:5).
- "Though the fig tree should not blossom, nor fruit be on the vines, the produce of the olive fail and the fields yield no food, the flock be cut off from the fold and there be no herd in the stalls, yet I will rejoice in the Lord; I will take joy in the God of my salvation. God, the Lord, is my strength; he makes my feet like the deer's; he makes me tread on my high places" (Hab. 3:17–19).
- "Though he slay me, I will hope in Him" (Job 13:15).
- "For the Lord God is a sun and shield; the Lord bestows favor and honor. No good thing does he withhold from those who walk uprightly" (Ps. 84:11).
- "What then shall we say to these things? If God is for us, who can be against us? He who did not spare his own Son but gave Him up for us all, how will he not also with Him graciously give us all things? ... Who shall separate us from the love of Christ? Shall tribulation, or distress, or persecution, or famine, or nakedness, or danger, or sword? ... In all these things we are more than conquerors through Him who loved us. For I am sure that neither death nor life, nor angels nor rulers, nor things present nor things to come, nor powers, nor height nor depth, nor anything else

in all creation, will be able to separate us from the love of God in Christ Jesus our Lord" (Rom. 8:31–32, 35, 37–39).

I choose to believe God is good in all things. Everything He does is first for His glory and then my ultimate good. There is never anything that happens that falls outside these two truth statements, regardless of how I perceive them in the moment. Even though the pain may be intense, God's purpose is to make me rely on Him because He raises the dead, as Paul wrote in 2 Corinthians 1:8–11.

> We were so utterly burdened beyond our strength that we despaired of life itself. Indeed, we felt that we had received the sentence of death. But that was to make us rely not on ourselves but on God who raises the dead. He delivered us from such a deadly peril, and he will deliver us. On Him we have set our hope that he will deliver us again.

Trust God. Believe Him. Flee to His side for refuge, comfort, and strength.

Chapter 11

WHEN AND HOW TO TERMINATE A MINISTER

. . . .

After chapter 10, it is right to consider the other side of church conflict, the congregation. Sadly, there are more quarrels in churches than people realize. My goal in what follows is for those who find themselves involved in a difficult church/minister situation to have a few guidelines so as to not defame the name of Christ in their conduct. As it is written, "Whatever happens, conduct yourself in a manner worthy of the Gospel of Christ."[424]

Jonathan Edwards, America's greatest theologian and pastor, credited as a central figure in the First Great Awakening, was fired by his congregation after twenty-three years of service, and 90 percent of the congregation voted against him. The reason for termination? His position that only believers should partake in the Lord's Supper.[425] The 230 who voted against him seem to have forgotten Hebrews 13:17, "Obey your leaders and submit to them, for they are keeping watch over your souls, as those who will have to give an account. Let them do this with joy and not with groaning, for that would be of no advantage to you."

Church/minister relationships are not good in America. Every month, seventeen hundred ministers leave the ministry[426] with an additional thirteen hundred terminated from all denominations.[427] Five years after finishing seminary, 50 percent of graduates will have left the ministry.[428] Most students entering seminary, including extension centers, choose not to become pastors because they have seen what churches do to pastors and the problems in churches.[429] Instead, they seek staff positions in larger churches or become church planters and missionaries.[430]

Behind every statistic is a story. When congregants want a minister to leave, they say things like, "He's not a good leader," "His organizational skills are lacking," "I'm not getting fed," "He doesn't visit enough," "He isn't a people person," "We need new ideas and a new direction," or "He's not a good fit for us." When people want a minister to leave, any reason is as good as another is, and the more reasons the better. Sadly, the minister's proficiency in fulfilling his call is largely ignored.

There are times when ministers should be terminated. And much like divorce, sometimes ending the minister-church relationship is the only option because of the hardness of human hearts.[431] There are three situations when termination of a minister is absolutely called for.

- When they bring disrepute on Christ by teaching or preaching heresy[432]
- When they bring disrepute on Christ by engaging in immoral behavior
- When they bring disrepute on Christ by laws in an egregious manner[433]

The purpose of this section is not about justifiable reasons to terminate a minister, but to examine a biblical process when termination is being considered. Because several congregations terminated the pastor prior to me (and having been asked to resign myself), I have observed the fallout of bad and improper decisions churches made when ending a minister's tenure. I have contemplated better ways that congregations could have conducted themselves if termination could not have been avoided. My prayer is that what follows will be of help to some who find themselves in difficult church situations.

Of First Importance

The most significant people to address a difficult situation with a minister are opinion leaders and/or respected elected leaders of the church: elders, deacons, and/or a personnel team member. Their first position should be, regardless of the accusation, to give the minister the benefit of the doubt as innocent. Even if the accusation seems credible, the minister should be believed because of his position, one who is worthy of double honor. "Let the elders who rule well be considered worthy of double honor, especially those who labor in preaching and teaching. Do not admit a charge against an elder except on the evidence of two or three witnesses" (1 Tim. 5:17, 19).

Because the minister is worthy of double honor, when a church member is criticizing or attacking a minister, including if another ministerial staff is participating, church leaders should approach him or her quickly to address his or her accusations to maintain the peace and unity of the congregation. For them not to do this is to avoid their call.[434] If an accusation is entertained, it must be from a credible witness, not hearsay, and then investigated thoroughly. The minister must be given an opportunity to give his or her side of the story, answer any accusations, and face his accuser(s). After all, if criminals are seen as innocent until proven guilty, allowed to face their accusers, and given fair representation for their defense, should not a minister of the gospel be granted more as one who is "worthy of double honor"?[435]

Joe McKeever, a well-respected pastor in the Southern Baptist Convention, has written many articles, one of which appeared in *SBC Today* regarding terminating a minister.[436] He asks church leaders to answer seven questions, after which he comments, "So, church leader, think this thing through. What kind of church do you want yours to become?" The following is a synopsis of his questions:

- Are you doing this in obedience to Christ, or is this just something you want done?

- Are you willing to stand before the Lord at judgment and take full responsibility for doing this?
- Have you brought in outside counsel (more than one person)?
- Has the pastor been able to present his or side of the matter before a responsible, nonjudgmental group?
- Have you checked your church's constitution and bylaws to make sure you are doing things right? (Note: I would add, "Have you searched Scripture to honor God in the process? A good start is the Golden Rule.)
- Have you rushed into this?
- Are you willing to tell the full story to the next pastor you consider bringing in?

Prayerfully and honestly answering these questions is a good starting point before seeking to force any minister to resign. The stakes are too high not to be careful and cautious. Remember what Jesus said to Saul on the road to Damascus, "Saul. Saul. Why are you persecuting me?"[437] when it comes to the treatment of ministers who are brothers and sisters in Christ.[438]

God will not allow an unfaithful minister to abuse his bride. He will chastise, discipline, and correct the minister if needed. The Chief Shepherd loves His church passionately and will not allow them to be neglected or treated harshly by anyone, especially a minister. With this in mind, make sure you consider seriously the following scriptures:

- "Respect those who labor among you and are over you in the Lord and admonish you, and to esteem them very highly in love because of their work" (1 Thess. 5:12–13).
- "Let the elders who rule well be considered worthy of double honor, especially those who labor in preaching and teaching" (1 Tim. 5:17).
- "Obey your leaders and submit to them, for they are keeping watch over your souls, as those who will have to give an

account. Let them do this with joy and not with groaning, for that would be of no advantage to you" (Heb. 13:17).
- "Touch not my anointed ones, do my prophets no harm" (1 Chr. 16:22).

So what should be done when a minister does something resulting in church conflict? What should church leaders do when a minister is hurting the congregation but his or her conduct is not immoral, unethical, breaking the law, or teaching heresy? Is the membership just to grin and bear it until he or she moves, retires, or dies? There are at least four things that can be done consistent with Hebrews 13:17b, "Let them do this with joy and not with groaning."

Pray

Pray for the minister, don't prey on them. This is God's will for His glory and your good. You might be surprised how God will change a minister or a situation when you pray diligently for them.

Encourage

Ministers mostly hear problems, complaints, and life difficulties. It is refreshing to have someone encourage and build them up. Send a card, and smile when you see them. Do this particularly when times are tumultuous. And don't forget the minister's wife as part of this process.[439]

Affirm

When they do something well, tell them. When they do something right, pat them on the back. A positive word of affirmation goes a long way to transform difficult situations.

Help

Find ways to help the minister be successful in fulfilling the call. Critics look for reasons to undercut the minister and then condemn him or her to anyone who'll listen. Do not criticize the minister to anyone. Do not allow anyone to criticize the minister in your presence. Consciously choose to talk to people, not about them. If you're not part of the solution, you are part of the problem.

Now let's consider a few things that church members can do when they find themselves in a difficult situation with ministers or staff. Keep in mind, "Nothing tests our obedience to Christ like conflict."[440]

When there is conflict, the question becomes not so much how the circumstance came about, but rather, "Will all involved conduct themselves in manner consistent with God's Word to glorify Him and address the situation?" If all are not devoted to restoration, mercy, repentance, and forgiveness, they have annulled the gospel before the congregation and community they are called to reach. If brothers and sisters in Christ will not work toward reconciliation, they have invalidated the credibility of their witness and should either repent or withdraw from positions of leadership in the church.

There are redemptive and helpful things that church leaders can do when there are staff problems. As Pricilla and Aquila helped Apollos,[441] as Paul helped Peter,[442] and as Barnabas[443] encouraged people to help two ladies in Philippians 4:2–3, it is important that leaders help the minister be successful. Thus, there are precedents in Scripture for coming alongside to help those who are having difficulties.

In 1 Samuel 2:30, it is written, "God honors those who honor Him." Regardless of what the minister does or how he or she conducts himself or herself, God will honor a congregation that seeks to be graciously redemptive in how they deal with a minister in a conflicted situation. It is written, "Whatever happens, conduct yourself in a manner worthy of the gospel,"[444] which applies to congregations and their leaders as much as it does to ministers. God will discipline those who terminate ministers for improper reasons or an inappropriate manner. God will honor and bless congregations that honor God by being gracious, loving, and merciful in difficult staff situations. Now I have a few more suggestions:

- DO NOT ambush a minister by having a group sit him or her down, recount everything he or she has done wrong, and impose what they've decided to do as a result.
- DO NOT include people who are a minister's adversaries in discussions with the minister.
- DO NOT have ultimatums, a letter of dismissal, or a severance package ready when meeting with a minister. Such things are not gracious, redemptive, helpful, or productive.
- DO approach the process with an attitude of humility, mercy, reconciliation, restoration, and forgiveness. The goal is to glorify God throughout in everything that takes place.[445]

From Matthew 18:15–18, have a person who loves the minister (and the minister knows this person loves him or her), go to him or her in private and talk with him or her one-on-one. This person must be honest with the minister about the gravity of the situation and the issues at hand. This person must be humble as he or she engages the minister in love consistent with Galatians 6:1–2.[446] The goal is to find solutions and correct problems (restoration) so as to continue a viable ministry for the church and minister's future. The goal of meeting is not to lay the groundwork for termination. Denominational workers are not the best ones to facilitate this process because they are not objective, and 90 percent of the time, they side with the congregation.[447]

"If anyone is caught in any transgression, you who are spiritual should restore Him in a spirit of gentleness. Keep watch on yourself, lest you too be tempted. Bear one another's burdens, and so fulfill the law of Christ" (Gal. 6:1–2). Paul is clear that the goal is always restoration to be done in a gentle manner. Interactions with ministers should always be conciliatory rather than confrontational or accusatory. The default objective must be toward healing rather than termination. Not only that, the one talking to the minister must have examined himself or herself first, which should at least include ("keep watch on yourself"):

- He or she must glorify God in all things.
- He or she must protect the reputation of Christ, the faith, and the church.
- He or she should make sure there is not a log in his or her own eye (Matt. 7:3–5).
- He or she must meet the goal of restoring effectiveness to the minister's ministry and personhood.
- He or she must be willing to help the minister ("bear one another's burdens").
- He or she must evaluate if there have been previous good faith attempts to help the minister. If this is not the case, then they should be attempted before anything else is done.
- He or she must do everything in keeping with the call to show love and the Golden Rule.

After going through this checklist diligently, then he or she can prayerfully engage the minister with respect and humility.

Early in the process, consider the possibility of a staff member needing personal help. He or she may be hurting and wounded in an area of his or her life you are not aware of. He or she might need encouragement or help for a difficult situation in his or her life being manifested in strained work relationships. There was a time in my ministry when I needed help with personal problems outside of the church context. Had I received help, I may have been able to minister more effectively. I don't blame the congregation, but looking back, it might have been helpful. Do everything you can to restore and redeem all involved.

If after attempts to help the minister and he or she is unwilling to change or get help, it is necessary to follow through with the rest of Matthew 18 by bringing him or her before a group representative of the church as a last resort. The manner in which this is done should be humble, merciful, gracious, and loving. This group should hear the matter and follow the recommendation of those who have tried to help the minister.

Answer this question: If those involved in a situation are all Christians who read the same Bible, pray to the same God, and are led by the same Holy Spirit, how can they not come to an agreement that embraces repentance, forgiveness, reconciliation, and restoration for God's glory? About disagreements in a congregation, Paul wrote in 1 Corinthians 6:1–7,

> When one of you has a grievance against another, does he dare go to law before the unrighteous instead of the saints? Or do you not know that the saints will judge the world? And if the world is to be judged by you, are you incompetent to try trivial cases? Do you not know that we are to judge angels? How much more, then, matters pertaining to this life! So if you have such cases, why do you lay them before those who have no standing in the church? I say this to your shame. Can it be that there is no one among you wise enough to settle a dispute between the brothers, but brother goes to law against brother, and that before unbelievers? To have lawsuits at all with one another is already a defeat for you. Why not rather suffer wrong? Why not rather be defrauded?

The minister is not the only person to which Matthew 18 applies. Churches will deal with a minister to the point of termination or forcing him or her to resign, which is church discipline by the way, while allowing worse sin in the congregation. It is not right to allow members to be gossips, divisive, liars, drunks, adulterers, thieves, and all kinds of other things but terminate a minister for lesser causes. Matthew 18 applies to all church members, not just ministers.

My prayer in this section is for church leaders who are not part of the ministerial staff to give serious consideration to the implications, results, consequences, and fallout when terminating a minister for improper reasons or terminating him or her ungraciously. My goal is for those who participate in such an event to still hear from Jesus one day, "Well done, good and faithful servant!" I pray the reader will always conduct himself or herself in a manner worthy of the gospel, even in the most difficult of times.

Discussion Questions

- What are your thoughts about the author's view of terminating a minister?
- What have been your experiences when a minister left under less than favorable circumstances?
- Are you willing to apply Hebrews 10:32–34 if your minister comes under fire? Why or why not?

Reflection 11: Praying Properly

While evaluating my prayer life not long back, I realized I was functionally treating God like an errand boy. Too many times, I asked God for deliverance from suffering. I wanted something from Him or for Him to do something for me. I had assumed my requests were in sync with God and His will. I took for granted that my heart's desire was the same as His. Thinking about these things led me to three passages of Scripture that applied to my ruminations:

- "And this is the confidence that we have toward him, that if we ask anything according to His will he hears us" (1 John 5:14).
- "You do not have, because you do not ask. You ask and do not receive, because you ask wrongly, to spend it on your passions. You adulterous people! Do you not know that friendship with the world is enmity with God?" (James 4:2b–4).
- "We do not know what to pray for as we ought, but the Spirit himself intercedes for us with groanings too deep for words. And he who searches hearts knows what is the mind of the Spirit, because the Spirit intercedes for the saints according to the will of God" (Rom. 8:26–27).

It is a hard to accept that doing something good (praying) can be done with the wrong motivation and therefore be ineffectual and possibly sinful. I don't like admitting I have, in essence, treated God as a hired errand boy, but I have and then wondered why my requests weren't answered.

Why do I ask God for whatever I ask Him? If it isn't for His name to be glorified, magnified, praised, and worshiped, but rather for me to get a blessing, be delivered from evil or pain, or get anything not having to do with exalting God, I have become a spiritual adulterer more concerned with myself than God.[448] It hurts to admit that, but it's true. For my prayer to be consistent with God's will, it must first be all about Him. Then I remembered when Jesus was to be crucified, how He was deeply troubled emotionally, and how He prayed.

> "Now is my soul troubled. And what shall I say? 'Father, save me from this hour?' But for this purpose I have come to this hour. Father, glorify your name." Then a voice came from heaven: "I have glorified it, and I will glorify it again" (John 12:27–29).

My current practice is to ask God to glorify His name and be magnified in the midst of whatever I am going through. I ask for His will to be done, whatever it may be. I ask Him to use me however He deems best for Him to be lifted up. Consequently, I have found "the peace that passes all understanding (guards) my heart and mind in Christ Jesus."[449] He conforms my heart to be content with Him alone.

Consider making Jesus' prayer from John 12 the desire of your heart in prayer, trusting Him.

Chapter 12

NOW WHAT?

On the other side of every mountain is a valley, and eventually, storm clouds follow sunny days. Chances are, you will encounter adversity to some degree in the future. Likewise, someone close to you will also encounter adversity. Now is the time to prepare so you can "count it all joy."

Just because we hear, see, or read something once, it doesn't mean we will remember or embrace it. That is probably true now that you have finished reading *Dancing in the Dungeon*. Because you or someone you know will go through difficulty in the future, the following suggestions are for you to consider now that you have finished reading *Dancing in the Dungeon*.

Application

Look at the people around you. God has put one or more who are struggling in ways similar to how you have suffered. He has placed them there because of 2 Corinthians 1:3–4, 6, for you to be used by Him to comfort them the way He has comforted you.

> Blessed be the God and Father of our Lord Jesus Christ, the Father of mercies and God of all comfort, who comforts us in all our affliction, so that we may be able to comfort those who are in any affliction, with the comfort with which we ourselves are comforted by God ... If we are comforted, it is for your comfort,

which you experience when you patiently endure the same sufferings that we suffer.

Suggestions

1. Read this book again. This time, highlight things you want to remember.
2. Go back to chapters that "scratched your itch." Meditate on the Scripture truths, and note the Bible references in your copy of God's Word.
3. Reexamine sections of chapters that stood out to you so you can become more familiar with them. You may need them again for yourself or to encourage someone else.
4. Form a group to read through this book together and discuss it. One or two chapters a week should be enough to fill an hour or so for mutual encouragement.
5. Don't give this book away but keep it handy as a future reference to read again in difficult times.
6. If you think this book is worthy, get a couple extra copies to give to those who you know who are going through difficulties for God to comfort them.

Finally, write out your own theology of encouragement. Write out what you believe about God from His Word. Write down the passages you will hang your hat on in good times and bad. Then commit them to memory by driving them deep into your heart so you will live to honor his name.

God bless you, and may He grant you the ability to dance in the dungeon for His glory!

AFTERWORD

. . . .

One of the main purposes of *Dancing in the Dungeon* is for my children and their families to have a resource to process and deal with the suffering I know they will all encounter one day. Thus, my conclusion is written first to them and then for others. I hope the reader will understand.

Amy and Austin, Trey and Hailey, Britton and Missy, remember, "But for the grace of God." There is no doubt in my mind that if God so chose to, He could remove His hand of protection, and I would break, being crushed to powder in an instant. The only thing that prevents such a happening at any moment is the grace and mercy of God. I take solace in the fact that God controls what comes into my life, and He will control whatever comes into yours.[450] No matter how hard or difficult life is, know that it would be worse but for the grace of God. Along with that thought, affirm Job 13:15, "Though he slay me, still I will hope in him!"

Prepare your heart before the day of adversity comes because if you fail in that day, your faith is weak.[451] Get to know God and love Him so much that His glory is more important than your ease or comfort, your health or well-being, or your life or that of your family. Love the Lord your God with all your heart, soul, mind, and spirit. Walk with the one who died for you every day. Talk with Him often. Read what He has written to you (Scripture). Worship Him often privately and corporately.

Drive deep into your soul and that of your family that God loves you all so much that He does not allow anything into your life that does not glorify Him and is ultimately good for you. God loves you so much that He is making sure you are becoming more like His Son every day. He loves you so much that nothing can snatch you out of His hand.[452] He loves you so much that there is nothing that can separate you from His love. God will not withhold anything good from you, ever.[453] So make sure you understand all of life's events in terms of who God is, not who God is in terms of life's events.

Your mom and I constantly pray for you all. We pray that God will make you more like His Son in whatever way He deems best. We pray God will make you more loving, merciful, patient, gracious, forgiving, and humble. We pray that He will use you in whatever way most glorifies Him. We pray that you will be able to handle and process suffering in a manner that glorifies God and results in your joy.

Jesus didn't suffer so you wouldn't suffer, but so that when you suffer, you would be like Him.[454] May He make it so in your life, along with your children's and grandchildren's.

To God be the glory.

Dad

APPENDIX A

"I Asked the Lord That I Might Grow"

Words by John Newton, Olney Hymns (London: W. Oliver, 1779):

I asked the Lord that I might grow, In faith and love and every grace, Might more of His salvation know, And seek more earnestly His face...

Twas He who taught me thus to pray, And He I trust has answered prayer, But it has been in such a way, As almost drove me to despair...

I hoped that in some favored hour, At once He'd answer my request, And by His love's constraining power, Subdue my sin and give me rest...

Instead of this, He made me feel, The hidden evils of my heart, And let the angry powers of hell, Assault my soul in every part...

Yea more with His own hand He seemed, Intent to aggravate my woe, Crossed all the fair designs I schemed, Humbled my heart, and laid me low...

Lord, why is this I trembling cried, Wilt Thou pursue Thy worm to death? "Tis in this way" The Lord replied, "I answer prayer for grace and faith"...

"These inward trials I employ, From self and pride to set thee free, And break thy schemes of earthly joy, That thou mayest find thy all in Me."

Note: On Tuesday, January 15, 2013, I was depressed and angry with myself, others, and, as much as it grieves me to write this, God.

I felt as though once again the rug had been pulled from under me unjustly. In the midst of my hurt, I had been given great hope about a matter, only to have it dashed. I prayed, and God restored my hope, only for it to be dashed a second time. And that's when anger, mixed with hurt from the previous event, started becoming fury and bitterness. After a text message that morning telling me of yet one more deep wound to my heart, my anger spiraled even deeper.

While thinking over these things, I couldn't understand the words to a song I had downloaded, so I found the lyrics to read while the song played. I read the words while the song played, and God's Spirit moved on me in a powerful way. For several hours (7:30 to 12:45 p.m.), all I did was listen to the song, weep, and ask God for forgiveness for my attitude of anger and bitterness. The picture above is the chair I was sitting in when God broke me and began healing me of deep hurt and anger.

Link… http://www.youtube.com/watch?v=nMKaUzNU38w (As of 11/13/2013)

ABOUT THE AUTHOR

·················

Ron Ethridge has been married to Pam since November 10, 1984, and resides in Muscle Shoals, Alabama. They have three married adult children: Amy with Austin, Trey with Hailey, and Britton with Missy. Ron graduated from Samford University with a bachelor of science, New Orleans Baptist Theological Seminary with a master of divinity, and Beeson Divinity School of Samford University with a doctor of ministry degree. He served as senior pastor from 1989 to 2012 for churches in Mississippi and Alabama. Presently, he is founder of Redemption Ministry with the goal to help, encourage, and comfort those who are struggling with a special affinity for those in ministry. He also leads Redemption Fellowship of the Shoals.

ENDNOTES

1. 2 Corinthians 1:3–7 is the foundation passage for *Dancing in the Dungeon*.
2. Romans 3:10–18
3. Ephesians 3:12–21
4. Until I have been beaten, stoned, whipped, and killed, I'm not willing to say that I have suffered for the gospel in light of the apostle's suffering (2 Cor. 11:23–29).
5. My dad was not saved even though he was a pastor. He hopefully came to Christ six weeks before he died thirty-nine years later.
6. My dream was to play football on scholarship for a major college, which I was able to do for two years. Then a series of events resulted in leaving the team and moving back home to live with my parents. In hindsight, figuring out God's purpose in this event began my journey to understand and process trials from a biblical perspective.
7. As of January of 2014, I have served five churches as senior pastor, one as an interim, over a twenty-three-year span.
8. Two of the three split as a result of firing the pastor prior to me. The timeline for these churches has been changed so they are not in the chronological order in which I served them to somewhat protect their identities.
9. I was the interim pastor for sixteen months.
10. I realized in this congregation that things may have looked good from the outside, but inside, there were serious problems beginning with distrust and integrity of these staff members.
11. Only the pastor immediately before me was able to leave after a long tenure. Prior to him, the church had fired the

pastor and split. I chose to resign in hopes of preventing this congregation having yet another ugly and public church fight in the community that would defame the name of Jesus. The pastor after me was terminated.

12 This was told to me by a man who served this church as pastor in 1953. Later, during a difficult time in my ministry there, a state worker told me the congregation had a reputation in the state as a perpetually conflicted congregation. I had been previously warned by a friend that the church was hard on ministers.

13 Romans 2:24

14 This was because the deacons removed a sign from the church cemetery for me to take to him. He had dedicated the church cemetery to his family without church approval.

15 This was deeply offensive and came from a former pastor who I thought understood ministry's difficulties.

16 All these accusations were untrue.

17 This was affirmed by a state worker who sought to bring clarity to the situation, and this was the main situation that ultimately resulted in choosing to resign as pastor.

18 The state worker called this person and demanded a retraction from the personnel team chairman because it was untrue. The personnel team chairman did not retract his accusation, which contributed to me choosing to resign.

19 Later, this staff member revealed he had been recording personal conversations with staff secretly, which the personnel team chose not to address when it was brought to their attention.

20 This is true. I have never preached Baptist doctrine. I have preached whatever is in Scripture as I came to it. Each time this accusation was made, it was because I preached with same passion John 3:16 with Ephesians 1:11, 2 Peter 3:9 with Romans 9:15–16, and Matthew 11:25–27 with Matthew 11:28–32.

21 At least one member of the search team was always involved in the situations described, except for the first church I served.

This was particularly difficult because I usually was closest to members of search teams that called me to a congregation.

22 To their credit, two congregations agreed to give me six- and seven-month severance of full salary and benefits, even if I found another place to serve as pastor, with an additional three months of health insurance and retirement. One congregation allowed me to stay in the parsonage for up to six months if I desired and pay for all my moving expenses anywhere within the state. God is good.
23 John 10:10–b
24 Genesis 38:24-31
25 Online dictionaries: Merriam-Webster, Oxford Dictionary, and Wikipedia.
26 Mark 10:29–30; Philippians 1:29; Romans 5:3–5, 8:17–18; 2 Corinthians 1:5; Philippians 3:8; Hebrews 5:7–8; 2 Corinthians 12:10
27 2 Corinthians 1:3–7
28 Hebrews 12:11
29 Hebrews 4:12
30 2 Corinthians 1:3–7
31 1 Corinthians 2:16
32 2 Peter 1:3–4; Luke 24:45
33 Connie Wiles, as told by her husband Charlie on November 15, 2013
34 Luke 22:31–32
35 John 7:38
36 Larry Crabb, "Finding God"
37 Tim Keller
38 Acts 5:12–42
39 Acts 5:19
40 Acts 5:33
41 Acts 5:40
42 John Piper, *Desiring God* (Random House, 2011), 168.
43 2 Corinthians 1:3–7

44. Isaiah 46:9–10; Psalm 84:11; Romans 8:18, 31b–32, 37–39
45. Isaiah 48:11
46. Luke 22:31–32
47. Romans 8:28
48. Romans 8:29
49. Romans 8:31–32
50. Psalm 84:11
51. Hebrews 13:8
52. Ephesians 3:20
53. Ibid.
54. Job 42:1–2, 5–6
55. Luke 10:38–42
56. Psalm 10:1, 22:1, 42:9, 43:2, 44:23–24, 74:1, 74:11, 88:14
57. Hebrews 4:16
58. Philippians 2:12, "Work out your own salvation" means working the gospel into every area of life. It means having the gospel drive thoughts, attitudes, and actions.
59. Mark 6:31 (NIV)
60. Romans 8:1
61. Philippians 4:13
62. Psalm 37:4
63. Proverbs 3:5
64. Romans 8:28
65. Romans 8:26–27
66. My dad and I studied the Bible several nights every week for years after my conversion. I obtained a master of divinity from New Orleans Baptist Theological Seminary and earned a doctor of ministry degree from Beeson Divinity School of Samford University.
67. Ligon Duncan, Timothy Keller, John MacArthur, and John Piper
68. Ryan Whitley, who has been a dear friend, pastor, and confidant since 1979; his brother Rhett, a friend since 1978, and Randy Bush, another insightful brother in ministry

69 2 Peter 3:16b
70 Timothy Keller, *Walking with God through Pain and Suffering* (Dutton, 2013), 13–14.
71 Ibid, 31.
72 In my ministry to hurting and wounded ministers (Redemption Ministry), I have found that many of them do not have a solid theology regarding how to process suffering in a biblical manner that glorifies God. Because ministers fall short in this area, it is doubtful those they're called to disciple will have a biblical perspective on suffering.
73 Romans 8:28–29
74 I met with him personally. He knew intellectually the plan of salvation but refused to be saved. I asked him if he knew what would happen if he died without Jesus, and he said, with tears streaming down his face, "I'll burn in hell forever. But you have to want to be saved, and I don't."
75 E.M. Bounds, Classic Collections on Prayer; Chapter 5, "Prayer and Trouble," page 128.
76 Philippians 1:6, 2:13 with Romans 8:29, "He … predestined to be conformed to the image of his Son."
77 2 Corinthians 6:10–a
78 Philippians 4:4–9, 11–12
79 1 John 4:8, 16
80 Psalm 73:1
81 Matthew 7:9–11
82 Isaiah 55:8–9
83 Romans 8:32
84 Psalm 84:11
85 Daniel 4:35
86 The first person to tell me, "You are in good company," was my friend Ryan Whitley. I have returned to his comment many times and have used those exact words with many others since 2004.
87 Esther 4:15–16

88. Mark 6:14–29
89. Revelation 6:9–11
90. Luke 10:19–20
91. Philippians 1:29
92. Hebrews 12:8
93. Romans 8:29
94. John 15:20
95. Philippians 2:13
96. Philippians 1:6
97. John 11:17, 43–44
98. Luke 9:23
99. 1 Peter 4:12–14
100. 1 Corinthians 10:31
101. Pam is my wife.
102. 1 Corinthians 4:3–5
103. 2 Timothy 2:7
104. Philippians 4:7
105. *Through the Gates of Splendor* (Tyndale, 1981), 268–269, 273.
106. Jeremiah 31:34; Hebrews 8:12, 10:15–17
107. Miroslav Volf, *Exclusion and Embrace.*
108. My dad and his brother
109. Matthew 6:14–15, 18:32–35
110. Matthew 6:15; Ephesians 4:32
111. Matthew 18:21–22; Luke 17:3–4
112. 2 Corinthians 1:3–7
113. Consider the only way to be of any earthly good is to be heavenly minded.
114. John 3:12; 1 Corinthians 2:9
115. Job 7:13–21, 10:18–19; Jonah 4:3
116. Matthew 24:31; 1 Corinthians 15:52
117. Revelation 1:10, 4:1
118. 1 Thessalonians 4:16
119. 1 Corinthians 15:51–52
120. 1 Thessalonians 4:17

121. Matthew 24:30, 26:64; Revelation 1:7
122. James 4:14
123. Luke 16:22
124. 1 Corinthians 15:51–55
125. Matthew 24:30–31; 1 Thessalonians 4:16–18
126. Psalm 116:15
127. Revelation 21:3
128. Luke 16:25
129. 1 John 3:2
130. John 14:1–4
131. Revelation 21:25
132. Revelation 22:2
133. Revelation 21:21
134. Ibid.
135. Revelation 4:8–11
136. Revelation 22:1–5
137. Revelation 2:17
138. 1 Corinthians 6:9–10
139. "Amazing Grace," "A Mighty Fortress Is Our God," "Holy, Holy, Holy," and so forth
140. Maranatha is translated "Oh Lord, come!" in 1 Corinthians 16:22–b.
141. Acts 17:24–25; Psalm 50:12, 15; Mark 10:45
142. Isaiah 6:3; Revelation 4:6–8
143. 2 Timothy 2:12; Revelation 20:6
144. Louisville, Kentucky, December 2012
145. 1 Corinthians 12:11
146. Ephesians 1:11
147. 1 Corinthians 4:2
148. Matthew 25:21
149. Hebrews 13:8
150. Genesis 18:14; Isaiah 59:1; Matthew 17:20, 19:26; Luke 1:37, 18:27; Ephesians 3:20
151. Philippians 1:6, 2:13

152. Psalm 119:11
153. Hebrews 2:1
154. 2 Corinthians 1:8–10
155. Ephesians 1:11
156. Philippians 1:29
157. Romans 8:28 (NASB)
158. Isaiah 46:9–10
159. Along with Job 23:13
160. Matthew 26:52–56, 11:25–27; John 12:37–40; Acts 13:48
161. Luke 11:11–13; Romans 8:31–32
162. Matthew 11:25–27; John 12:37–40
163. Acts 17:30
164. Matthew 7:7
165. Philippians 4:6
166. Proverbs 3:5
167. Matthew 27:46
168. Matthew 17:5–6
169. Exodus 32
170. 1 Samuel 13:11–14
171. Exodus 33:15
172. Hebrews 13:5
173. John 10:28–29
174. Romans 8:29
175. Romans 8:37–39
176. 1 Corinthians 10:13
177. Ibid.
178. Matthew 12:20
179. Philippians 4:7; John 14:27
180. Psalm 84:11
181. Philippians 1:6
182. Philippians 2:13
183. Hebrews 13:5
184. *George Mueller of Bristol*, by Authur Tappen Pierson, page 16. James Nisbet. London, 1899.

185 Philippians 4:4
186 Dr. Tim Keller
187 Colossians 1:17
188 Romans 8:16
189 Matthew 11:15; Mark 4:9, 23; Luke 8:8, 14:35
190 Romans 1:19–20
191 Matthew 11:25; 16:17
192 Matthew 7:7
193 From the hymn, "How Firm A Foundation"
194 Hebrews 4:12
195 Job 38:4–41
196 Romans 9:20
197 This was from a state worker where I served.
198 *By God's grace*, the church paid off all debt, operated in the black every year, grew from 315 to over 600 in attendance, and built a 3.2 million-dollar facility.
199 Matthew 6:8; 7:7, 11; 21:22
200 Matthew 7:11
201 Romans 8:29
202 Psalm 119:67, 70
203 Matthew 6:33
204 Matthew 11:28–30
205 1996 Atlanta Promise Keepers Conference
206 Acts 14:22
207 Hebrews 2:10, 5:8
208 Philippians 1:29
209 2 Corinthians 1:5, 12:9–10
210 1 Peter 2:21
211 Romans 8:31–32; Psalm 84:11
212 Hebrews 12:11
213 Luke 9:23; James 4:7
214 Proverbs 3:5
215 Matthew 6:10
216 Philippians 4:7

217 Psalm 119:11
218 John 4:13–14
219 1 John 5:14–15
220 Jeremiah 31:31–34
221 Job 13:15
222 Deuteronomy 6:5; Matthew 22:37; Mark 12:30
223 Matthew 6:33
224 1 Corinthians 10:31
225 Philippians 1:27
226 Matthew 5:13–16
227 Romans 12:18
228 1 Kings 8:57–58; Psalm 119:33–36, 38; 1 Corinthians 15:10
229 Philippians 1:6, 2:13
230 1 Peter 1:15–16
231 John 15:5–b
232 Hebrews 6:1–3
233 Isaiah 6:1–4
234 John 12:27–29
235 John 17:20–21
236 Matthew 27:45
237 Matthew 27:41–44
238 Luke 22:44
239 Luke 14:26–27
240 Job 13:15
241 Galatians 1:15–16
242 Acts 9:15–16
243 Suffering in and of itself is not proof of God's displeasure or that a believer is being punished by Him. All of God's anger toward each believer was dealt with on the cross when He punished Jesus. Therefore, everything believers experience is from God's heart of love.
244 2 Corinthians 4:17
245 2 Corinthians 1:9
246 Ibid.

247. 1 Corinthians 10:13–14, particularly verse 14
248. 1 John 5:14
249. Philippians 3:4b–11
250. Romans 8:29
251. Romans 8:18
252. Philippians 1:6, 2:13
253. 1 John 4:4
254. Romans 8:26–27
255. James 4:1–8
256. 2 Corinthians 1:3–7 paraphrased
257. 1 Samuel 16:33
258. 2 Samuel 12:18–20
259. Matthew 26:30
260. Acts 16:23–25
261. Psalm 119:11
262. Matthew 6:6
263. Matthew 14:23; Mark 6:46; Luke 9:28
264. Luke 2:36–37
265. 1 Samuel 1:24–2:11
266. Daniel 6:10
267. James 5:16
268. 1 Thessalonians 5:17
269. Most of these songs can be accessed through YouTube or purchased on iTunes.
270. Romans 12:1
271. 1 Corinthians 6:19
272. Isaiah 55:1
273. Philippians 4:7
274. John 21:15–17
275. Ephesians 1:11
276. Psalm 84:11; Romans 8:32
277. Genesis 50:20
278. Genesis 41:46
279. Genesis 41:34–36

280 1 Corinthians 10:11
281 1 Samuel 2:30
282 2 Corinthians 5:7; Romans 1:17; Galatians 2:20, 3:11; Hebrews 10:38
283 Matthew 12:20
284 Matthew 26:47–50
285 John 13:18–19; Luke 22:21–22; Matthew 26:24
286 See Foreword, *My Afflictions for Your Comfort*
287 When I brought this as a response to church leadership, it was denied.
288 Proverbs 24:17
289 Philippians 1:27
290 John 17:17
291 2 Samuel 12:7–a
292 Romans 8:29
293 1 John 4:17–18
294 Luke 9:23
295 Romans 8:29
296 Philippians 1:6, 2:13
297 Matthew 25:23
298 Proverbs 17:17, 18:24, 27:6
299 Hebrews 12:4–11
300 Philippians 2:12–13
301 Genesis 50:20
302 Acts 4:27–28
303 Luke 9:23; Hebrews 12:14
304 Hebrews 12:10
305 Romans 8:28–29
306 Hebrews 12:9
307 Hebrews 12:11
308 1 Corinthians 3:10–15
309 Romans 8:29
310 Hebrews 12:11
311 Romans 5:15–17, 20–21; Ephesians 2:8–9

312 Matthew 5:21–26
313 His conduct included performing illegal abortions, marital infidelity, drunkenness, and a host of many other things.
314 Galatians 6:7–8; Proverbs 6:27–28
315 1 John 1:9
316 Galatians 5:16–18, 24–25
317 Psalm 103:11–14
318 Genesis 28:16
319 Matthew 26:69–75
320 John 18:10
321 Luke 22:62
322 Luke 22:61
323 John 21:15–18
324 Matthew 27:3–10
325 Matthew 26:75
326 Matthew 26:35
327 John 21:15–17
328 Ibid.
329 Acts 2:37–47
330 Luke 22:31–32
331 1 John 1:9
332 Romans 8:38–39
333 2 Samuel 11:1–12:25
334 2 Samuel 12:10–14
335 2 Samuel 12:14–a
336 Hebrews 11:5–6, 10b–11
337 Luke 19:1–10
338 Genesis 9:20–21
339 Genesis 12:1–4, 11–13
340 Numbers 20:6–11
341 Acts 13:22; 2 Samuel 12:7–9
342 Matthew 16:16, 26:75; Acts 2:14–47; Galatians 2:11–14
343 2 Corinthians 12:1–2, 12:8–9; Romans 7:15
344 1 John 1:9

345 Hebrews 6:1–3
346 Matthew 10:22b
347 1 Thessalonians 4:3
348 Romans 8:29; Philippians 1:6, 2:13
349 1 Corinthians 12:4–11
350 Acts 13:48
351 Hebrews 6:1–3
352 1 Corinthians 15:10
353 Philippians 3:12–14
354 2 Timothy 3:1–7 (note especially verses 5 and 7)
355 Confirming salvation is also strongly encouraged in chapter 10.
356 Matthew 12:34
357 Matthew 7:23
358 1 Corinthians 1:10
359 1 Corinthians 1:26–31
360 1 Corinthians 3:1–9
361 1 Corinthians 3:16–17
362 1 Corinthians 4:6–7
363 1 Corinthians 5:1–2
364 1 Corinthians 5:9–13
365 1 Corinthians 6:1–8 (This was giving the faith a bad reputation in the city.)
366 1 Corinthians 6:15–20
367 1 Corinthians 7
368 1 Corinthians 8:11–13
369 1 Corinthians 11:17–32 (Death 11:30)
370 False conversions are warned about in Scripture. Everyone thought Judas was surely a believer, but he wasn't. Jesus Himself gave warning in Matthew 7:21–23. In Acts 8:18–23, Peter told Simon the Sorcerer that he had not been saved even though he "believed and was baptized" (Acts 8:13). In James 2:19, it is written that even the demons "believe" and yet tremble because they are not saved.
371 Matthew 7:21–23

372 Spurgeon's Morning and Evening, October 17, AM.
373 Isaiah 41:10
374 Hebrews 13:5
375 Matthew 8:23–27
376 Matthew 10:29–31
377 Matthew 14:23–27
378 Luke 12:29–34
379 Acts 18:9–10
380 Philippians 1:21
381 Philippians 1:15–17
382 Philippians 4:11–12
383 Philippians 1:29
384 Philippians 1:14
385 Philippians 1:29
386 2 Timothy 2:7
387 1 Peter 5:6–11
388 http://www.youtube.com/watch?v=nMKaUzNU38w or http://pastorron7.wordpress.com/grow-newton
389 Dale Huff, Alabama Baptist Director of the Office of LeaderCare and Church Administration
390 These included informal groups of church leaders, deacons, personnel teams, and other church members.
391 1 Corinthians 10:31
392 James 3:1
393 Matthew 25:40; Acts 9:4; Matthew 18:10
394 Colossians 4:6
395 Ephesians 1:11; Isaiah 46:9–10
396 Matthew 5:44
397 Galatians 6:1
398 Ephesians 4:32
399 Acts 7
400 Matthew 5:11–12
401 1 Corinthians 4:3–5
402 Luke 19:17

403. Mark 6:7–13; John 6:70–71; Matthew 7:21–23
404. 1998 NOBTS class notes, "American Christianity," Dr. Claude Howe
405. 2 Corinthians 13:5
406. Acts 26:1–29
407. Too many young men choose to enter the ministry because others tell them they are called by God. No one's parent, grandparent, aunt, uncle, or church member can call a person to vocational ministry. Only God calls people into ministry. See 1 Romans 1:1, Corinthians 1:1, Galatians 1:15, and 2 Timothy 1:9.
408. 2 Timothy 2:7
409. Rhett Whitley, quoting A. L. Williams.
410. Colossians 3:1–3
411. Matthew 25:21
412. Hebrews 12:11
413. 2 Timothy 1:13; Philippians 3:17
414. Romans 2:24
415. Isaiah 46:9–10; Psalm 84:11; Romans 8:18, 31b–32, 37–39
416. Isaiah 48:11
417. Luke 22:31–32
418. Romans 8:28
419. Romans 8:29
420. Romans 8:31–32
421. Isaiah 55:8–9
422. Romans 8:28 (NASB)
423. Tim Keller
424. Philippians 1:27
425. http://gratefultothedead.wordpress.com/2009/12/07/preacher-in-the-hands-of-an-angry-church-the-fall-of-jonathan-edwards/
426. http://www.9marks.org/blog/dont-make-your-pastor-statistic *quoted from the Schaeffer Institute.*
427. Ibid.

428 http://www.nytimes.com/2006/03/17/national/17seminary.html?pagewanted=all&_r=0
429 Dr. Ron Pate, Director of Birmingham New Orleans Baptist Theological Seminary Extension Center
430 Ibid.
431 Matthew 19:8–9
432 Romans 2:24; 2 Samuel 12:14
433 Such as theft, stealing, or other similar crimes
434 Acts 6:1–3
435 This paragraph is written because, in one church, I was not afforded these things even though I requested them more than once, with a secular judge being party to the discussions as a church leader. Then I presented these things to the deacon body without any response. I have talked with many ministers who have been terminated or forced to resign without the "due process" described here.
436 http://sbctoday.com/2011/10/01/before-you-terminate-the-pastor/
437 Acts 9:4–5
438 Matthew 25:40, 45
439 1 Thessalonians 5:11; Hebrews 10:25
440 Dr. Dale Huff, Alabama Baptist Director of the Office of LeaderCare and Church Administration
441 Acts 18:26
442 Galatians 2:11–14
443 Acts 15:36–41
444 Philippians 1:27 (NIV)
445 1 Corinthians 10:31
446 1 John 4:7, 11, 19–21
447 Charles Chandler, Ministering to Ministers Foundation, "It is easier for the church to find another minister than work through the restoration and healing process. Congregations pay the denominational worker's salary so they are more likely to side with them rather than the minister."

[448] James 4:2b–4
[449] Philippians 4:7
[450] 1 Corinthians 10:13
[451] Proverbs 24:10
[452] John 10:28–30
[453] Psalm 84:11
[454] Amy Carmichael

CPSIA information can be obtained at www.ICGtesting.com
Printed in the USA
LVOW06s0836290514

387633LV00002B/2/P